Effortless Diabetic Air Fryer Recipes Cookbook for Beginners

Enjoy Simple, Healthy, and Delicious Meals for Easy Diabetes Management - With Pictures

by Delores Pyle

Copyright © by Delores Pyle

Introduction

Welcome to "Effortless Diabetic Air Fryer Recipes for Beginners," a treasure trove of simple, healthy, and utterly delicious recipes designed specifically for those managing diabetes. Whether you are newly diagnosed, a caretaker, or simply looking to infuse your meals with a healthier twist, this cookbook by Delores Pyle is your gateway to a revitalized kitchen experience.

In this book, we emphasize ease without sacrificing flavor. You will discover that managing your diet through an air fryer is not just about reducing fats and sugars—it's about creating mouthwatering meals that you look forward to eating. Each recipe has been carefully crafted to ensure that it meets the nutritional needs of diabetics, promoting stable blood sugar levels without skimping on taste.

Why an air fryer? Because it's an excellent tool for anyone looking to prepare meals quickly and with minimal oil. This cooking method preserves the natural flavors and textures of foods, making it easier to enjoy the richness of ingredients without unhealthy additives.

From hearty breakfasts to satisfying dinners and a few delightful snacks in between, every recipe includes step-by-step instructions, complete with high-quality pictures that make cooking as easy as following along. Whether craving a crispy snack or a comforting dinner, you'll find recipes that suit every mood and occasion.

Moreover, this cookbook helps you understand how simple dietary adjustments can significantly impact your health. Alongside the recipes, you'll find tips for diabetic management, nutritional facts for every dish, and advice on how best to utilize your air fryer to its fullest potential.

Join Delores Pyle on this culinary journey that promises to feed your stomach and nourish your soul. Let's turn the simple act of cooking into a joyful celebration of health and flavor.

Table of Contents

CHAPTER 01: Welcome to Your Diabetic-Friendly Air Fryer Journey

Welcome to the world of diabetic-friendly air frying! If you've just unboxed your new air fryer or are considering dusting off an older one, you're in for a delightful culinary adventure. This "Diabetic Air Fryer Cookbook for Beginners" is designed to introduce you to the basics of air frying and guide you through creating delicious and suitable meals for managing diabetes.

Air frying is a revolutionary cooking technique that offers a healthier alternative to traditional frying methods. By using hot air to cook your meals, the air fryer creates dishes that are crispy on the outside and tender on the inside, all with minimal use of cooking oil. This not only helps reduce fat intake—a crucial aspect in diabetic diet management—but also helps control calories without compromising on taste and texture.

Why Air Fry for Diabetics?

Managing diabetes requires careful consideration of food choices, particularly in carbohydrate and sugar intake, to maintain balanced blood sugar levels. The air fryer shines here by allowing you to enjoy your favorite foods, like crispy chicken, fries, and even desserts, in a way that fits your dietary needs.

The magic of air frying lies in its ability to impart a deep-fried taste and texture, which can make transitioning to a healthier diet more enjoyable and sustainable. With this cookbook, you'll discover that eating doesn't mean giving up on the foods you love but transforming them into healthier versions that support your health goals.

Getting Started with Your Air Fryer

Before diving into the recipes, it's essential to familiarize yourself with your air fryer. Most models come with a basket or tray where you place your food and simple controls to adjust the temperature and cooking time.

Here's a quick rundown on getting started:

- **Preheating**: Some recipes will call for preheating your air fryer. This ensures a consistent cooking environment, much like preheating an oven.

- **Spacing**: Keep the basket neat to ensure even cooking. Air needs to circulate the food for it to crisp up properly.

- **Shaking or Flipping**: For items like fries or vegetables, shaking the basket halfway through cooking or flipping them over will help achieve an even crispness.

- **Temperature Control**: Air fryers cook food at high speed, so it's sometimes necessary to adjust temperatures or cooking times based on your specific model or the recipe's needs.

Your First Set of Recipes

This cookbook provides a range of recipes, from breakfasts to desserts, tailored to be diabetic-friendly and easy for any beginner to master.

Here's a preview of what you can expect:

- **Breakfast**: Start your day with a plate of cinnamon-spiced apple rings or savory breakfast frittatas, all made quickly and without the excess oil of pan-frying.

- **Lunch**: Enjoy crispy tofu wraps or a classic tuna melt, showcasing how the air fryer can create textures that are perfect for a midday meal that's both satisfying and healthy.

- **Dinner**: Explore flavors with dishes like garlic and herb chicken thighs or zesty lime shrimp, proving that a diabetic diet can still be rich in taste and variety.

- **Snacks**: Whip up kale chips or almond and cinnamon roasted chickpeas for a guilt-free snack that keeps your energy levels stable and your palate happy.

- **Desserts**: Yes, you can still indulge! Bake an apple crisp or some peach empanadas to satisfy that sweet tooth responsibly.

Each recipe includes nutritional information to help you keep track of your carbohydrate and sugar intake, alongside tips for getting the best results with your air fryer.

Tips for Success

Managing diabetes effectively with your diet involves more than just choosing the right foods; it's transforming your lifestyle. Here are a few tips to keep in mind:

1. **Stay Informed**: Understand how foods affect blood sugar levels and adjust your cooking methods and ingredients accordingly.

2. **Be Consistent**: Try to maintain a regular meal schedule to avoid significant fluctuations in your blood sugar levels.

3. **Experiment**: Use your air fryer to experiment with new vegetables and protein sources to keep your meals exciting and nutritious.

Welcome aboard this health, flavor, and innovation journey with your air fryer. Here's to delicious meals that are kind to your body and taste buds!

CHAPTER 02: Start Smart: Diabetic-Friendly Breakfasts

Recipe 01: Toast with Avocado and Fried Egg

Start your day with this nutritious and satisfying avocado and egg toast made quick and easy in your air fryer. It's perfect for a diabetic-friendly breakfast that's as delicious as healthy.

> **Prep Time:** 5 minutes

> **Cook Time:** 8 minutes

> **Serves:** 1

Ingredients:

- ➢ 1 slice of whole-grain bread
- ➢ 1/2 ripe avocado

- ➢ 1 egg
- ➢ Salt and pepper to taste
- ➢ Optional garnish: red pepper flakes, fresh parsley

Instructions:

1. Preheat the air fryer to 370°F (188°C).
2. Place the bread slice in the air fryer basket and cook for 3 minutes until slightly toasted.
3. Meanwhile, slice the avocado and spread it evenly over the toasted bread.
4. Crack the egg into a small bowl and carefully slide it onto the avocado toast. Season with salt and pepper.
5. Return the basket to the air fryer and cook for another 5 minutes or until the egg is cooked to your liking.
6. Garnish with red pepper flakes and fresh parsley if desired.

Nutritional Facts (Per serving):

- ❖ Calories: 289
- ❖ Carbohydrates: 19g
- ❖ Protein: 10g
- ❖ Fat: 20g
- ❖ Fiber: 7g
- ❖ Sugar: 2g

Enjoy your vibrant and healthful avocado and egg toast, a perfect balance of protein, healthy fats, and fiber to kickstart your morning.

Recipe 02: Healthy Vegan Banana Blueberry Muffins

Whip up a batch of these delightful vegan banana blueberry muffins for a quick, heart-healthy breakfast. Packed with fruit and flavor, they're perfect for a diabetic-friendly morning treat everyone can enjoy.

Prep Time: 10 minutes

Cook Time: 15 minutes

Serves: 4

Ingredients:

- ➢ 2 ripe bananas, mashed
- ➢ 1 cup blueberries
- ➢ 1 1/2 cups whole wheat flour
- ➢ 1/2 cup almond milk
- ➢ 1/4 cup coconut oil, melted

- ➢ 1/4 cup maple syrup
- ➢ 1 tsp baking powder
- ➢ 1/2 tsp cinnamon
- ➢ 1/4 tsp salt

Instructions:

1. Preheat the air fryer to 320°F (160°C).
2. Combine the mashed bananas, almond milk, melted coconut oil, and maple syrup in a large bowl.
3. Sift in the flour, baking powder, cinnamon, and salt. Stir until just combined.
4. Fold in the blueberries gently to avoid crushing.
5. Spoon the batter into silicone muffin cups, filling each about three-quarters full.
6. Place the cups in the air fryer basket and cook for 15 minutes or until a toothpick inserted into the center comes out clean.
7. Let cool for a few minutes before serving.

Nutritional Facts (Per serving):

- ❖ Calories: 295
- ❖ Carbohydrates: 51g
- ❖ Protein: 5g
- ❖ Fat: 9g
- ❖ Fiber: 6g
- ❖ Sugar: 16g

Start your day with these deliciously tender and moist vegan banana blueberry muffins, which are ideal for a quick, nutritious breakfast or a sweet afternoon snack.

Recipe 03: Crispy Turkey Bacon Strips

Indulge in the crispy, savory goodness of turkey bacon made effortlessly in your air fryer. This recipe offers a healthier alternative to traditional bacon, perfect for a diabetic-friendly breakfast that doesn't sacrifice flavor.

Prep Time: 2 minutes

Cook Time: 10 minutes

Serves: 2

Ingredients:

- ➤ 8 strips of turkey bacon

Instructions:

1. Preheat the air fryer to 360°F (182°C).

2. Arrange the turkey bacon strips in a single layer in the air fryer basket. Depending on the size of your air fryer, you may need to work in batches.

3. Cook for 10 minutes, flipping the strips halfway through until the bacon is crispy.

4. Remove the bacon strips from the air fryer and place them on a paper towel-lined plate to drain any excess fat.

Nutritional Facts (Per serving):

❖ Calories: 70

❖ Carbohydrates: 0g

❖ Protein: 6g

❖ Fat: 5g

❖ Fiber: 0g

❖ Sugar: 0g

Enjoy these perfectly crispy turkey bacon strips. They are a simple yet satisfying addition to any breakfast plate and provide a lean protein option without the extra grease.

Recipe 04: Mini Quiches with Spinach

Enjoy a delightful, easy-to-make breakfast with these mini quiches featuring fresh spinach and a touch of cheese. Perfect for a diabetic-friendly meal, they're baked in your air fryer for a quick, nutritious start to your day.

Prep Time: 15 minutes

Cook Time: 15 minutes

Serves: 4

Ingredients:

➢ 4 large eggs

➢ 1 cup fresh spinach, chopped

➢ 1/4 cup milk (or dairy-free alternative)

➢ 1/4 cup shredded cheddar cheese (or dairy-free alternative)

➢ 1/4 cup diced onions

- ➤ Salt and pepper to taste
- ➤ Cooking spray

Instructions:

1. Mix eggs, milk, salt, and pepper in a large bowl.

2. Stir in the spinach, cheese, and onions.

3. Spray the muffin cups with cooking spray and evenly distribute the quiche mixture among them, filling each about three-quarters full.

4. Preheat the air fryer to 300°F (150°C).

5. Place the filled muffin cups in the air fryer basket and cook for 15 minutes or until the quiches are set and lightly golden on top.

6. Remove the mini quiches from the air fryer and let them cool for a few minutes before serving.

Nutritional Facts (Per serving):

- ❖ Calories: 150
- ❖ Carbohydrates: 3g
- ❖ Protein: 11g
- ❖ Fat: 10g
- ❖ Fiber: 1g
- ❖ Sugar: 2g

These mini quiches are a tasty and convenient breakfast choice and an excellent way to incorporate more greens into your diet. Enjoy them hot for a satisfying and nutritious meal.

Recipe 05: Brioche French Toast with Blueberries and Almonds

Savor the sweet richness of brioche French toast, enhanced with the vibrant flavors of blueberries and almonds. This diabetic-friendly air fryer recipe transforms a classic breakfast into a healthful treat that's both easy to make and delicious.

Prep Time: 10 minutes

Cook Time: 8 minutes

Serves: 2

Ingredients:

- ➤ 4 slices of brioche bread
- ➤ 2 large eggs
- ➤ 1/3 cup almond milk
- ➤ 1/2 teaspoon vanilla extract

- ➢ 1/2 teaspoon cinnamon
- ➢ 1/2 cup fresh blueberries
- ➢ 1/4 cup sliced almonds
- ➢ Sugar-free maple syrup (for serving)
- ➢ Cooking spray

Instructions:

1. Whisk the eggs, almond milk, vanilla extract, and cinnamon in a shallow bowl.

2. Dip each slice of brioche bread into the egg mixture, ensuring both sides are well coated.

3. Spray the air fryer basket with cooking spray and place the soaked bread slices in a single layer.

4. Cook at 360°F (182°C) for 4 minutes, flip the bread slices, and cook for another 4 minutes until golden and crispy.

5. Serve the French toast hot, topped with blueberries, sliced almonds, and a drizzle of sugar-free maple syrup.

Nutritional Facts (Per serving):

- ❖ Calories: 345
- ❖ Carbohydrates: 45g
- ❖ Protein: 14g
- ❖ Fat: 12g
- ❖ Fiber: 3g
- ❖ Sugar: 8g

This delightful brioche French toast offers a luxurious yet health-conscious way to start your day. It combines the indulgence of rich brioche with the nutritious boost of blueberries and almonds. Enjoy it as a special breakfast or a brunch treat.

Recipe 06: Cinnamon Apple Chips

Delight in the crispy sweetness of cinnamon apple chips, a simple yet flavorful snack perfect for a diabetic-friendly diet. These chips offer a guilt-free way to enjoy a delicious treat anytime.

Prep Time: 10 minutes

Cook Time: 20 minutes

Serves: 2

Ingredients:

- ➤ 2 large apples, thinly sliced
- ➤ 1 teaspoon ground cinnamon
- ➤ Cooking spray

Instructions:

1. Preheat your air fryer to 320°F (160°C).

2. Lightly spray the air fryer basket with cooking spray.

3. Arrange apple slices in a single layer in the basket; you may need to work in batches.

4. Sprinkle the apple slices with ground cinnamon.

5. Cook for 10 minutes, flip the slices, and cook for another 10 minutes until the apple chips are crispy and lightly browned.

6. Let them cool to become even crispier before serving.

Nutritional Facts (Per serving):

❖ Calories: 95

❖ Carbohydrates: 25g

❖ Protein: 0.5g

❖ Fat: 0.3g

❖ Fiber: 4.4g

❖ Sugar: 18.9g

Enjoy these aromatic cinnamon apple chips as a light breakfast or a healthy snack. They're an excellent choice for curbing your sweet cravings while keeping your blood sugar in check.

Recipe 07: Sausage and Peppers Frittata

Enjoy a robust start to your day with this sausage and peppers frittata, made simple and delicious in your air fryer. This recipe combines savory flavors and hearty ingredients, making it a perfect diabetic-friendly meal for breakfast or brunch.

Prep Time: 10 minutes

Cook Time: 18 minutes

Serves: 4

Ingredients:

➤ 4 large eggs

➤ 1/2 cup milk

➤ 1/2 cup diced turkey sausage

➤ 1/2 cup bell peppers, mixed colors, chopped

➤ 1/4 cup shredded cheddar cheese

- ➤ Salt and pepper to taste
- ➤ Cooking spray

Instructions:

1. Whisk together eggs, milk, salt, and pepper in a bowl.

2. Stir in the sausage, bell peppers, and cheddar cheese.

3. Spray the air fryer basket with cooking spray. Pour the frittata mixture into the basket.

4. Cook at 360°F (182°C) for 18 minutes or until the frittata is set and golden on top.

5. Let it cool slightly before slicing and serving.

Nutritional Facts (Per serving):

- ❖ Calories: 180
- ❖ Carbohydrates: 3g
- ❖ Protein: 12g
- ❖ Fat: 13g
- ❖ Fiber: 0.5g
- ❖ Sugar: 2g

This sausage and pepper frittata is a filling and nutritious option for your morning meal. Its flavorful punch will keep you satisfied throughout the morning.

Recipe 08: Diet Crumble with Oatmeal, Cinnamon and Pears

Whip up this delectable diet crumble with oatmeal, cinnamon, and pears to start your morning with sweetness. Perfectly diabetic-friendly, this air fryer recipe transforms simple ingredients into a delightful, comforting breakfast.

Prep Time: 10 minutes

Cook Time: 15 minutes

Serves: 2

Ingredients:

➢ 2 medium pears, peeled and chopped

➢ 1 cup rolled oats

➢ 1 tsp ground cinnamon

➢ 2 tbsp almond flour

➢ 1 tbsp coconut oil, melted

- ➢ 1 tbsp sugar-free maple syrup
- ➢ Cooking spray

Instructions:

1. Preheat the air fryer to 350°F (177°C).

2. Mix the chopped pears with cinnamon and sugar-free maple syrup in a bowl.

3. Combine rolled oats, almond flour, and melted coconut oil in another bowl to make the crumble topping.

4. Spray the air fryer basket with cooking spray. Layer the pear mixture at the bottom and top with the oatmeal crumble.

5. Cook for 15 minutes or until the topping is golden and crisp.

6. Serve warm.

Nutritional Facts (Per serving):

- ❖ Calories: 270
- ❖ Carbohydrates: 38g
- ❖ Protein: 4g
- ❖ Fat: 12g
- ❖ Fiber: 6g
- ❖ Sugar: 15g

Enjoy this heartwarming crumble, a delightful blend of flavors and textures that makes for a perfect, guilt-free start to your day.

Recipe 09: Egg Baked in Avocado with Salt and Pepper

Indulge in a simple yet stunning breakfast with eggs baked in avocado. This dish is eye-catching and packed with nutrients, making it a superb choice for anyone following a diabetic-friendly diet.

Prep Time: 5 minutes

Cook Time: 15 minutes

Serves: 2

Ingredients:

- ➢ 2 ripe avocados
- ➢ 4 small eggs
- ➢ Salt and pepper to taste
- ➢ Optional garnishes: chopped chives, paprika

Instructions:

1. Slice the avocados in half and remove the pits. Scoop out a bit more avocado to widen the holes.

2. Crack an egg into each avocado half—season with salt and pepper.

3. Preheat the air fryer to 350°F (177°C).

4. Place the avocado halves gently in the air fryer basket. Cook for 15 minutes or until the eggs are cooked to your desired doneness.

5. Garnish with chives and a sprinkle of paprika before serving.

Nutritional Facts (Per serving):

- ❖ Calories: 470

- ❖ Carbohydrates: 17g

- ❖ Protein: 14g

- ❖ Fat: 40g

- ❖ Fiber: 13g

- ❖ Sugar: 2g

Enjoy this rich and creamy egg baked in avocado for a nutritious and satisfying breakfast, perfect for a leisurely morning or an upscale brunch.

Recipe 10: Mushroom and Egg Burritos with Microgreens

Elevate your breakfast routine with these hearty mushroom and egg burritos topped with fresh microgreens. This diabetic-friendly recipe utilizes the air fryer for a quick, nutritious meal with flavor and good-for-your ingredients.

Prep Time: 10 minutes

Cook Time: 10 minutes

Serves: 2

Ingredients:

➤ 4 large eggs

➤ 1 cup sliced mushrooms

➤ 1/2 cup microgreens

➤ 2 whole wheat tortillas

➤ 1/4 cup shredded low-fat cheese

- ➢ Salt and pepper to taste
- ➢ Cooking spray

Instructions:

1. In a skillet, sauté the mushrooms until tender. Remove and set aside.

2. Whisk the eggs in a bowl and scramble them in the same skillet, seasoning with salt and pepper.

3. Lay the tortillas and evenly distribute the cooked mushrooms, scrambled eggs, and cheese.

4. Roll up the tortillas to form burritos.

5. Preheat the air fryer to 360°F (182°C). Spray the burritos lightly with cooking spray.

6. Cook in the air fryer for 5 minutes or until the tortillas are crisp and golden.

7. Serve topped with microgreens.

Nutritional Facts (Per serving):

- ❖ Calories: 345
- ❖ Carbohydrates: 28g
- ❖ Protein: 21g
- ❖ Fat: 17g
- ❖ Fiber: 4g
- ❖ Sugar: 3g

Enjoy these delicious and wholesome mushroom and egg burritos, a perfect start to your morning with the added freshness of microgreens. They're quick to make, fill, and energize your day.

Recipe 11: Keto Bagels with Cream Cheese

Indulge in the rich flavors of keto bagels topped with cream cheese, smoked salmon, and capers. This gourmet breakfast, perfect for a diabetic-friendly diet, brings a touch of luxury to your morning routine using your air fryer.

Prep Time: 15 minutes

Cook Time: 10 minutes

Serves: 2

Ingredients:

➢ 2 keto bagels

➢ 4 oz cream cheese, softened

➢ 4 oz smoked salmon

➢ 1 tablespoon capers

➢ 1/2 red onion, thinly sliced

- ➢ Fresh dill for garnish

Instructions:

1. Slice the keto bagels in half.

2. Preheat the air fryer to 360°F (182°C).

3. Place the bagel halves in the air fryer basket and toast for about 5 minutes until crisp.

4. Remove the bagels from the air fryer and let them cool slightly.

5. Spread each half with cream cheese. Top with smoked salmon, capers, and slices of red onion.

6. Garnish with fresh dill before serving.

Nutritional Facts (Per serving):

- ❖ Calories: 400

- ❖ Carbohydrates: 13g

- ❖ Protein: 25g

- ❖ Fat: 28g

- ❖ Fiber: 1g

- ❖ Sugar: 4g

Start your day with these decadent keto bagels. They combine the smoothness of cream cheese with the savory taste of smoked salmon and the tangy bite of capers—a truly satisfying low-carb delight.

Recipe 12: Smoked Salmon with Capers on Toast

Start your morning with a sophisticated yet simple dish: smoked salmon with capers on toast. This diabetic-friendly recipe uses your air fryer to crisp the bread perfectly, offering a delightful contrast to the smooth salmon.

Prep Time: 5 minutes

Cook Time: 3 minutes

Serves: 2

Ingredients:

- ➤ 2 slices of whole-grain bread
- ➤ 4 oz smoked salmon
- ➤ 1 tablespoon capers
- ➤ 2 teaspoons olive oil
- ➤ Fresh dill for garnish

> ➢ Lemon wedges for serving

Instructions:

1. Preheat the air fryer to 360°F (182°C).

2. Brush each slice of bread lightly with olive oil.

3. Place the bread in the air fryer basket and cook for about 3 minutes, until crispy.

4. Remove the toast from the air fryer, and top each slice with smoked salmon and capers.

5. Garnish with fresh dill and serve with a wedge of lemon.

Nutritional Facts (Per serving):

❖ Calories: 210

❖ Carbohydrates: 15g

❖ Protein: 15g

❖ Fat: 10g

❖ Fiber: 2g

❖ Sugar: 2g

Enjoy this elegant smoked salmon on toast, a light yet satisfying dish that combines crispiness with creamy and zesty flavors, perfect for a nutritious and upscale breakfast.

Recipe 13: Corned Beef Hash with Sweet Potato and Carrots

Savor a comforting and hearty start to your day with this Corned Beef Hash featuring sweet potatoes and carrots. This dish delivers all the classic flavors you love in a diabetic-friendly format.

Prep Time: 10 minutes

Cook Time: 20 minutes

Serves: 4

Ingredients:

- 1 cup cooked corned beef, diced
- 1 large sweet potato, peeled and diced
- 1 cup carrots, diced
- 1 medium onion, diced
- 1/2 teaspoon paprika

- ➤ Salt and pepper to taste
- ➤ 2 tablespoons olive oil

Instructions:

1. In a large bowl, mix sweet potato, carrots, onion, corned beef, paprika, salt, pepper, and olive oil until well combined.

2. Preheat the air fryer to 380°F (193°C).

3. Transfer the mixture to the air fryer basket, spreading it evenly.

4. Cook for 20 minutes, stirring halfway through, until the vegetables are tender and the corned beef is crispy.

5. Serve hot.

Nutritional Facts (Per serving):

- ❖ Calories: 230
- ❖ Carbohydrates: 23g
- ❖ Protein: 12g
- ❖ Fat: 10g
- ❖ Fiber: 4g
- ❖ Sugar: 6g

Delight in this delicious Corned Beef Hash with sweet potatoes and carrots, a wholesome and satisfying breakfast that energizes your mornings with balanced flavors and nutrients.

Recipe 14: Cheesy Broccoli Breakfast Casserole

Kickstart your day with this hearty Cheesy Broccoli Breakfast Casserole, made easy in your air fryer. This nutritious and delicious dish combines vibrant broccoli and melty cheese, perfect for a diabetic-friendly, fulfilling morning meal.

Prep Time: 10 minutes

Cook Time: 20 minutes

Serves: 4

Ingredients:

- ➢ 2 cups broccoli florets
- ➢ 6 large eggs
- ➢ 1 cup shredded cheddar cheese
- ➢ 1/2 cup milk
- ➢ 1/2 teaspoon garlic powder

- ➢ Salt and pepper to taste
- ➢ Cooking spray

Instructions:

1. Steam the broccoli until just tender, about 3-4 minutes, then chop into small pieces.

2. Mix eggs, milk, garlic powder, salt, and pepper in a large bowl.

3. Stir in the steamed broccoli and cheddar cheese.

4. Spray a baking dish that fits your air fryer with cooking spray. Pour the egg and broccoli mixture into the dish.

5. Preheat the air fryer to 360°F (182°C).

6. Place the dish in the air fryer and cook for 20 minutes until the casserole is set and the top is golden brown.

7. Let cool slightly before serving.

Nutritional Facts (Per serving):

- ❖ Calories: 290
- ❖ Carbohydrates: 6g
- ❖ Protein: 19g
- ❖ Fat: 21g
- ❖ Fiber: 1g
- ❖ Sugar: 2g

This Cheesy Broccoli Breakfast Casserole offers a warm, comforting start to your day. It's delicious layers of eggs, cheese, and broccoli make every bite a perfect balance of flavor and nutrition.

Recipe 15: Healthy Cauliflower Hash Browns

Reimagine your morning with these Healthy Cauliflower Hash Browns crafted in your air fryer for a delightful crunch. They're a fantastic low-carb, diabetic-friendly alternative to traditional hash browns, as nutritious as delicious.

Prep Time: 15 minutes

Cook Time: 15 minutes

Serves: 2

Ingredients:

- ➢ 2 cups cauliflower rice
- ➢ 1 small onion, finely chopped
- ➢ 1 large egg
- ➢ 1/4 cup almond flour
- ➢ 1/2 teaspoon garlic powder

- ➢ Salt and pepper to taste
- ➢ Cooking spray

Instructions:

1. Mix cauliflower rice, onion, egg, almond flour, garlic powder, salt, and pepper in a large bowl until well combined.

2. Form the mixture into small patties.

3. Preheat the air fryer to 375°F (190°C). Spray the air fryer basket with cooking spray.

4. Place the patties in the basket, ensuring they do not touch. Cook for 15 minutes, flipping halfway through, until golden and crispy.

5. Serve hot.

Nutritional Facts (Per serving):

- ❖ Calories: 160
- ❖ Carbohydrates: 14g
- ❖ Protein: 8g
- ❖ Fat: 8g
- ❖ Fiber: 4g
- ❖ Sugar: 5g

Enjoy these Healthy Cauliflower Hash Browns, a perfect start to your day with a satisfying crunch and loads of flavor, all while keeping your carb count in check.

CHAPTER 03: Healthy Lunchbox: Air Fryer Magic

Recipe 16: Toasted Tuna Melt Sandwich

Elevate your lunchtime with this Toasted Tuna Melt Sandwich, perfectly crispy and deliciously melty, thanks to your air fryer. This diabetic-friendly recipe combines simplicity and flavor for a satisfying midday meal that's both quick and healthy.

Prep Time: 5 minutes

Cook Time: 8 minutes

Serves: 1

Ingredients:

➤ 2 slices whole-grain bread

- ➤ 1 can (5 oz) tuna in water, drained
- ➤ 1 tablespoon low-fat mayonnaise
- ➤ 1 slice of low-fat cheese
- ➤ 1 tablespoon diced celery
- ➤ Salt and pepper to taste
- ➤ Cooking spray

Instructions:

1. Mix the tuna, mayonnaise, celery, salt, and pepper in a bowl.
2. Spread the tuna mixture on one slice of bread, top with a slice of cheese, and cover with the other.
3. Spray both sides of the sandwich lightly with cooking spray.
4. Preheat the air fryer to 360°F (182°C).
5. Cook the sandwich in the air fryer for 8 minutes, flipping halfway through, until the bread is toasted and the cheese is melted.
6. Serve hot.

Nutritional Facts (Per serving):

- ❖ Calories: 330
- ❖ Carbohydrates: 28g
- ❖ Protein: 25g
- ❖ Fat: 12g
- ❖ Fiber: 5g
- ❖ Sugar: 4g

Relish the comforting warmth of this Toasted Tuna Melt Sandwich, a deliciously crisp and melty treat that packs robust flavor into a simple, diabetic-friendly lunch option.

Recipe 17: Quinoa Stuffed Peppers with Corn and Basil

Enjoy a burst of flavors with Quinoa-Stuffed Peppers filled with corn and basil for a refreshing, nutritious lunch. This easy, diabetic-friendly recipe uses an air fryer to perfectly cook the peppers, maintaining their vibrant color and crisp texture.

Prep Time: 15 minutes

Cook Time: 10 minutes

Serves: 4

Ingredients:

- ➢ 4 bell peppers, tops cut off and seeds removed
- ➢ 1 cup cooked quinoa
- ➢ 1/2 cup corn kernels
- ➢ 1/4 cup chopped fresh basil

- ➢ 1/4 cup diced red onion
- ➢ 1/4 cup crumbled feta cheese
- ➢ 1 tablespoon olive oil
- ➢ Salt and pepper to taste

Instructions:

1. Combine the cooked quinoa, corn, basil, red onion, feta cheese, olive oil, salt, and pepper in a bowl.

2. Stuff the mixture into the hollowed-out bell peppers.

3. Preheat the air fryer to 350°F (177°C).

4. Place the stuffed peppers in the air fryer basket and cook for 10 minutes or until the peppers are tender and the filling is heated through.

5. Serve immediately.

Nutritional Facts (Per serving):

- ❖ Calories: 190
- ❖ Carbohydrates: 27g
- ❖ Protein: 6g
- ❖ Fat: 8g
- ❖ Fiber: 5g
- ❖ Sugar: 8g

Savor these deliciously fresh Quinoa Stuffed Peppers, a perfect blend of texture and taste, for a light, satisfying lunch packed with nutrition and easy to prepare.

Recipe 18: Chicken Veggie Wrap with French Fries

Wrap up your lunch with this Chicken Veggie Wrap with crispy air-fried French fries. This balanced meal delivers flavor and nutrition, using the air fryer to keep things light and diabetic-friendly.

Prep Time: 15 minutes

Cook Time: 20 minutes

Serves: 2

Ingredients:

- 2 whole wheat tortillas
- 2 chicken breasts, thinly sliced
- 1 cup mixed salad greens
- 1/2 cucumber, thinly sliced
- 1 carrot, julienned
- 1/2 bell pepper, julienned

- ➢ 2 tbsp low-fat Greek yogurt
- ➢ 1 tbsp olive oil
- ➢ 1 tsp lemon juice
- ➢ Salt and pepper to taste
- ➢ 2 medium potatoes, cut into fries
- ➢ Cooking spray

Instructions:

1. Preheat the air fryer to 380°F (193°C).

2. Toss the potato fries with olive oil and salt, then spread them in the air fryer basket. Cook for 18-20 minutes, shaking halfway through, until crispy.

3. While the fries cook, heat a skillet over medium heat with olive oil and cook the chicken with salt and pepper until golden and cooked through.

4. Mix the Greek yogurt with lemon juice, salt, and pepper to create a dressing.

5. Lay the tortillas and evenly distribute the salad greens, cucumber, carrot, bell pepper, and cooked chicken. Drizzle with yogurt dressing.

6. Roll up the tortillas tightly to enclose the filling.

7. Serve the wraps with the freshly air-fried French fries.

Nutritional Facts (Per serving):

- ❖ Calories: 540
- ❖ Carbohydrates: 55g
- ❖ Protein: 40g
- ❖ Fat: 20g
- ❖ Fiber: 8g
- ❖ Sugar: 8g

Enjoy your Chicken Veggie Wrap with a side of golden, crispy French fries— a satisfying, nutritious meal with wholesome ingredients and delightful flavors that keep you fueled throughout the day.

Recipe 19: Grilled Kofta Köfte Shish Kebab

Experience the rich flavors of the Middle East with these Grilled Kofta Kebabs, skillfully prepared in your air fryer. These kebabs are a diabetic-friendly delight that promises a feast of flavors.

Prep Time: 20 minutes

Cook Time: 10 minutes

Serves: 4

Ingredients:

- ➢ 1/2-pound ground lamb
- ➢ 1/2-pound ground beef
- ➢ 1 small onion, finely chopped
- ➢ 2 cloves garlic, minced
- ➢ 2 tablespoons chopped fresh parsley

- ➢ 1 teaspoon ground cumin

- ➢ 1 teaspoon paprika

- ➢ 1/2 teaspoon ground coriander

- ➢ Salt and pepper to taste

- ➢ Cooking spray

Instructions:

1. Combine ground lamb, beef, onion, garlic, parsley, cumin, paprika, coriander, salt, and pepper in a large bowl. Mix well.

2. Divide the mixture into long, thin kebabs around skewers.

3. Preheat the air fryer to 400°F (200°C).

4. Spray the air fryer basket with cooking spray. Place the kebabs in the basket, ensuring they do not touch.

5. Cook for 10 minutes, turning halfway through, until the meat is thoroughly cooked and slightly charred on the outside.

6. Serve hot.

Nutritional Facts (Per serving):

- ❖ Calories: 300
- ❖ Fat: 21g

- ❖ Carbohydrates: 3g
- ❖ Fiber: 1g

- ❖ Protein: 23g
- ❖ Sugar: 1g

Enjoy these Grilled Kofta Kebabs. They are a perfect blend of spices and succulent meat, making them a delightful and hearty choice for a satisfying and diabetes-friendly lunch.

Recipe 20: Fried Tofu Cheese with Broccoli

Dive into a fusion of flavors with this Fried Tofu Cheese dish, paired with broccoli, mushrooms, and a drizzle of teriyaki sauce. This quick, easy, diabetic-friendly meal is cooked in an air fryer for a healthier, delicious lunch.

Prep Time: 15 minutes

Cook Time: 15 minutes

Serves: 2

Ingredients:

➢ 1 block (14 oz) firm tofu, pressed and cubed

➢ 1 cup broccoli florets

➢ 1 cup sliced mushrooms

➢ 1/4 cup teriyaki sauce (low-sodium)

➢ 2 tablespoons olive oil

- ➢ Salt and pepper to taste
- ➢ Sesame seeds for garnish

Instructions:

1. Toss the tofu cubes with olive oil, salt, and pepper.
2. Preheat the air fryer to 380°F (193°C).
3. Place the tofu in the air fryer basket and cook for 10 minutes until crispy, shaking halfway through.
4. In the last 5 minutes, add the broccoli and mushrooms to the tofu in the air fryer and continue cooking.
5. Toss the tofu, broccoli, and mushrooms in teriyaki sauce once cooked.
6. Garnish with sesame seeds before serving.

Nutritional Facts (Per serving):

- ❖ Calories: 310
- ❖ Carbohydrates: 18g
- ❖ Protein: 20g
- ❖ Fat: 18g
- ❖ Fiber: 3g
- ❖ Sugar: 6g

Savor this delightful Fried Tofu Cheese with fresh veggies and savory teriyaki sauce. It's a perfect meal that blends taste with nutritional benefits, making it ideal for a satisfying and health-conscious lunch.

Recipe 21: Gourmet Beef Medallions with Potatoes and Mushrooms

Elevate your lunch with Gourmet Beef Medallions, expertly paired with potatoes and mushrooms for a filling, diabetic-friendly meal. This air fryer recipe delivers restaurant-quality taste with the convenience and health benefits of home cooking.

Prep Time: 15 minutes

Cook Time: 12 minutes

Serves: 2

Ingredients:

- ➤ 4 beef medallions, about 1 inch thick
- ➤ 2 large potatoes, sliced into rounds
- ➤ 1 cup sliced mushrooms
- ➤ 2 tablespoons olive oil

- ➢ 1 teaspoon garlic powder
- ➢ Salt and pepper to taste
- ➢ Fresh parsley, chopped for garnish

Instructions:

1. Brush the beef medallions with 1 tablespoon olive oil, then season with garlic powder, salt, and pepper.

2. Toss the potato slices and mushrooms with olive oil and a pinch of salt and pepper.

3. Preheat the air fryer to 400°F (200°C).

4. Place the beef medallions in the air fryer basket and cook for 6 minutes. Flip the medallions, add the potatoes and mushrooms around them, and cook for another 6 minutes or until the beef is cooked to your liking and the vegetables are tender.

5. Serve the beef medallions topped with parsley, accompanied by the potatoes and mushrooms.

Nutritional Facts (Per serving):

- ❖ Calories: 550
- ❖ Carbohydrates: 40g
- ❖ Protein: 35g
- ❖ Fat: 28g
- ❖ Fiber: 5g
- ❖ Sugar: 3g

Enjoy these succulent Gourmet Beef Medallions with perfectly air-fried potatoes and mushrooms. This luxurious yet simple dish brings a touch of elegance to your daily dining without compromising your dietary needs.

Recipe 22: Pita Stuffed with Chicken, Beans and Lettuce

Discover the delightful flavors in this Pita Stuffed with Chicken, Beans, and Lettuce. This wholesome lunch balances protein, fiber, and taste. This meal is not only diabetic-friendly but also quick and easy to prepare.

Prep Time: 10 minutes

Cook Time: 15 minutes

Serves: 2

Ingredients:

- ➢ 2 whole wheat pita breads
- ➢ 1 chicken breast, cooked and shredded
- ➢ 1/2 cup black beans, rinsed and drained
- ➢ 1 cup chopped lettuce
- ➢ 1/4 cup diced tomatoes

- ➢ 1/4 cup low-fat Greek yogurt

- ➢ 1 teaspoon ground cumin

- ➢ Salt and pepper to taste

Instructions:

1. Preheat the air fryer to 360°F (182°C).

2. Mix the shredded chicken with black beans, cumin, salt, and pepper.

3. Warm the pita bread in the air fryer for 2 minutes until slightly toasted.

4. Fill the pitas with the chicken mixture, lettuce, and tomatoes.

5. Top with a dollop of Greek yogurt.

6. Serve immediately for the best taste.

Nutritional Facts (Per serving):

- ❖ Calories: 340

- ❖ Carbohydrates: 45g

- ❖ Protein: 28g

- ❖ Fat: 6g

- ❖ Fiber: 7g

- ❖ Sugar: 4g

Enjoy this fresh and filling Pita Stuffed with Chicken, Beans, and Lettuce, a nutritious meal that keeps you energized and satisfied throughout the afternoon. Perfect for a quick yet balanced lunch!

Recipe 23: Fried Shrimp with Lemon and Sauce

Dive into the zesty flavors of Fried shrimp with Lemon and sauces, a delightful dish that's both diabetic-friendly and delectably crispy. This air fryer recipe offers a quick, healthy way to enjoy a seafood favorite without the extra oil.

Prep Time: 10 minutes

Cook Time: 8 minutes

Serves: 2

Ingredients:

- ➢ 1-pound shrimp, peeled and deveined
- ➢ 1 tablespoon olive oil
- ➢ 1 lemon, zested and juiced
- ➢ 1 teaspoon garlic powder
- ➢ Salt and pepper to taste

- ➤ 2 tablespoons low-sugar cocktail sauce

Instructions:

1. Toss the shrimp with olive oil, lemon zest, lemon juice, garlic powder, salt, and pepper.

2. Preheat the air fryer to 400°F (200°C).

3. Place the shrimp in the air fryer basket in a single layer. Cook for 8 minutes, shaking halfway through, until golden and crispy.

4. Serve hot with a side of cocktail sauce.

Nutritional Facts (Per serving):

- ❖ Calories: 220
- ❖ Carbohydrates: 3g
- ❖ Protein: 34g
- ❖ Fat: 8g
- ❖ Fiber: 0g
- ❖ Sugar: 1g

Enjoy the crisp, citrus-infused delight of these Fried shrimp, enhanced with a tangy sauce that makes for a perfect quick lunch or a light, flavorful meal any day.

Recipe 24: Mexican Wet Burrito with Red Enchilada Sauce

Savor the bold and vibrant flavors of this Mexican Wet Burrito, smothered in rich red enchilada sauce. This air fryer rendition lightens up the traditional recipe, making it a healthier, diabetic-friendly option without skimping on taste.

Prep Time: 15 minutes

Cook Time: 10 minutes

Serves: 4

Ingredients:

- 4 large whole wheat tortillas
- 1-pound lean ground beef
- 1 cup cooked brown rice
- 1 can (15 oz) black beans, rinsed and drained
- 1 cup shredded low-fat cheddar cheese
- 2 cups red enchilada sauce

- ➤ 1/2 cup diced onions
- ➤ 1/2 cup diced bell peppers
- ➤ 1 teaspoon cumin
- ➤ 1 teaspoon chili powder
- ➤ Salt and pepper to taste
- ➤ Fresh cilantro for garnish

Instructions:

1. In a skillet, cook the ground beef with onions, bell peppers, cumin, chili powder, salt, and pepper until the meat is browned.
2. Stir in black beans and cooked rice, heating through.
3. Spoon the mixture onto each tortilla, top with some cheese, and roll up tightly.
4. Preheat the air fryer to 360°F (182°C).
5. Place the burritos in the air fryer basket. Cook for 5 minutes until crisp.
6. Heat the enchilada sauce separately and pour over the air-fried burritos.
7. Garnish with fresh cilantro and serve hot.

Nutritional Facts (Per serving):

- ❖ Calories: 510
- ❖ Carbohydrates: 65g
- ❖ Protein: 36g
- ❖ Fat: 12g
- ❖ Fiber: 12g
- ❖ Sugar: 5g

Dive into this delectable Mexican Wet Burrito, a meal that combines the hearty goodness of beef and beans with the zest of enchilada sauce. It delivers a satisfying feast that keeps your health in check.

Recipe 25: Falafel Balls with Sour Cream Dipping

Indulge in the delicious crunch of Falafel Balls paired with a tangy sour cream dip. This air-fried version offers a healthier, diabetic-friendly alternative to the deep-fried favorite, ensuring you enjoy every bite without the guilt.

Prep Time: 20 minutes

Cook Time: 15 minutes

Serves: 4

Ingredients:

- 2 cups canned chickpeas, drained and rinsed
- 1 small onion, chopped
- 2 cloves garlic, minced
- 2 tablespoons fresh parsley, chopped
- 1 teaspoon ground cumin

- ➢ 1 teaspoon ground coriander
- ➢ Salt and pepper to taste
- ➢ 1/2 cup all-purpose flour (or chickpea flour for gluten-free)
- ➢ Cooking spray
- ➢ 1/2 cup sour cream
- ➢ 1 tablespoon lemon juice
- ➢ 1 teaspoon dried dill

Instructions:

1. Blend chickpeas, onion, garlic, parsley, cumin, coriander, salt, and pepper in a food processor until smooth.
2. Stir in the flour to form a dough-like consistency. Shape into small balls.
3. Preheat the air fryer to 360°F (182°C).
4. Lightly spray the falafel balls with cooking spray and place them in the air fryer basket. Cook for 15 minutes, turning halfway through, until golden and crisp.
5. Mix sour cream, lemon juice, and dill for the dipping sauce.
6. Serve the falafel hot with sour cream dip.

Nutritional Facts (Per serving):

- ❖ Calories: 260
- ❖ Carbohydrates: 33g
- ❖ Protein: 9g
- ❖ Fat: 11g
- ❖ Fiber: 6g
- ❖ Sugar: 5g

Enjoy these flavorful Falafel Balls with a refreshing sour cream dip. The perfect blend of taste and texture will satisfy your cravings while keeping your dietary needs in check.

Recipe 26: Fried Chicken with French Fries

Indulge in the timeless comfort of Fried Chicken with French Fries, now made healthier and diabetic-friendly using your air fryer. This classic combo delivers all the crispy goodness you crave with a fraction of the oil.

Prep Time: 15 minutes

Cook Time: 20 minutes

Serves: 4

Ingredients:

- ➢ 4 boneless, skinless chicken breasts
- ➢ 2 cups panko breadcrumbs
- ➢ 1 egg, beaten
- ➢ 1 tsp paprika
- ➢ 1 tsp garlic powder

- ➢ Salt and pepper to taste

- ➢ 4 medium potatoes sliced into fries

- ➢ Cooking spray

Instructions:

1. Season the chicken breasts with salt, pepper, paprika, and garlic powder.

2. Dip each breast in the beaten egg, then coat with panko breadcrumbs.

3. Spray the air fryer basket with cooking spray. Place the chicken and fries separately in the basket.

4. Cook at 380°F (193°C) for 20 minutes, turning the chicken and fries halfway through, until the chicken is golden and cooked and the fries are crispy.

5. Serve hot.

Nutritional Facts (Per serving):

- ❖ Calories: 410

- ❖ Carbohydrates: 53g

- ❖ Protein: 31g

- ❖ Fat: 9g

- ❖ Fiber: 4g

- ❖ Sugar: 3g

Enjoy this air-fried version of Fried Chicken with French Fries, a meal that satisfies your comfort food cravings while being mindful of your health. Perfect for a hearty lunch that is balanced with flavor and texture.

Recipe 27: Barbecue Point Steak with Artichoke Hearts

Savor the robust flavors of Barbecue Point Steak with Artichoke Hearts, a gourmet yet simple dish that combines succulent steak with the unique taste of artichokes in your air fryer. This diabetic-friendly meal doesn't skimp on satisfaction.

Prep Time: 10 minutes

Cook Time: 12 minutes

Serves: 2

Ingredients:

- ➢ 2-point steaks (approximately 6 oz each)
- ➢ 1 cup canned artichoke hearts, drained
- ➢ 2 tablespoons barbecue sauce (sugar-free)
- ➢ 1 tablespoon olive oil

- ➢ 1 teaspoon garlic powder
- ➢ Salt and pepper to taste

Instructions:

1. Rub each steak with olive oil, garlic powder, salt, and pepper.
2. Preheat the air fryer to 400°F (204°C).
3. Place the steaks in the air fryer basket and cook for 10 minutes, turning once halfway through.
4. Add the artichoke hearts to the basket in the last 2 minutes of cooking and brush the steaks with barbecue sauce.
5. Continue cooking until the steaks are done to your liking and the artichokes are heated.
6. Serve immediately.

Nutritional Facts (Per serving):

- ❖ Calories: 380
- ❖ Carbohydrates: 8g
- ❖ Protein: 34g
- ❖ Fat: 24g
- ❖ Fiber: 2g
- ❖ Sugar: 3g

Relish this delightful Barbecue Point Steak with Artichoke Hearts, a meal that's as nourishing as it is flavorful, perfect for a special lunch or a satisfying, healthy midday treats.

Recipe 28: Chinese Chicken Salad

Experience a burst of flavors with this Chinese Chicken Salad, a vibrant mix of shredded chicken, mandarin oranges, and crunchy noodles. This air fryer recipe is a colorful, diabetic-friendly lunch option that's both refreshing and satisfying.

Prep Time: 20 minutes

Cook Time: 10 minutes

Serves: 4

Ingredients:

- ➤ 2 cups cooked chicken breast, shredded
- ➤ 1 can (15 oz) mandarin oranges, drained
- ➤ 1 cup crunchy noodles
- ➤ 1 cup red cabbage, thinly sliced
- ➤ 1 cup Napa cabbage, thinly sliced

- ➢ 1/2 cup carrots, julienned

- ➢ 1/4 cup green onions, chopped

- ➢ 3 tablespoons low-sugar Asian dressing

- ➢ 1 tablespoon sesame seeds

- ➢ Salt and pepper to taste

Instructions:

1. Cook the chicken breast in the air fryer at 360°F (182°C) for 10 minutes or until fully cooked. Allow to cool, then shred.

2. Combine shredded chicken, mandarin oranges, red cabbage, Napa cabbage, carrots, and green onions in a large bowl.

3. Add the crunchy noodles and toss with the Asian dressing.

4. Season with salt and pepper, and sprinkle with sesame seeds.

5. Serve chilled for the freshest taste.

Nutritional Facts (Per serving):

- ❖ Calories: 235

- ❖ Carbohydrates: 25g

- ❖ Protein: 20g

- ❖ Fat: 7g

- ❖ Fiber: 3g

- ❖ Sugar: 10g

Dive into this Chinese Chicken Salad, a delectable and easy-to-make meal that combines crisp vegetables, tender chicken, and sweet oranges for a nutritious lunch that keeps your taste buds and health in check.

Recipe 29: Lamb Stewed with Potatoes

Savor the comforting flavors of Lamb Stewed with Potatoes, a hearty dish that combines tender lamb and earthy potatoes, cooked to perfection in your air fryer. This diabetic-friendly meal is simple yet robust, ideal for a satisfying lunch.

Prep Time: 15 minutes

Cook Time: 25 minutes

Serves: 4

Ingredients:

- ➤ 1-pound lamb shoulder, cut into cubes
- ➤ 4 medium potatoes, peeled and cubed
- ➤ 1 onion, chopped
- ➤ 2 carrots, sliced
- ➤ 2 cloves garlic, minced

- ➢ 2 cups beef broth (low sodium)
- ➢ 1 teaspoon rosemary
- ➢ 1 teaspoon thyme
- ➢ Salt and pepper to taste
- ➢ 2 tablespoons olive oil

Instructions:

1. Preheat the air fryer to 350°F (177°C).

2. Toss the lamb with salt, pepper, rosemary, and thyme in a bowl.

3. Heat olive oil in a pan over medium heat. Brown the lamb on all sides.

4. Place the browned lamb, potatoes, onion, carrots, garlic, and beef broth in the air fryer basket.

5. Cook for 25 minutes, stirring halfway through, until the lamb is tender and the potatoes are cooked.

6. Adjust seasoning if necessary and serve hot.

Nutritional Facts (Per serving):

- ❖ Calories: 410
- ❖ Carbohydrates: 30g
- ❖ Protein: 28g
- ❖ Fat: 20g
- ❖ Fiber: 4g
- ❖ Sugar: 3g

Enjoy this warm and filling Lamb Stewed with Potatoes, a nourishing dish that brings traditional comfort to your table with ease. It's a perfect choice for a cozy, nutritious meal.

Recipe 30: Asian Teriyaki Beef with Red and Yellow Bell Peppers

Immerse yourself in the vibrant flavors of Asian cuisine with this Teriyaki Beef dish. It features succulent beef, colorful bell peppers, and tender broccoli sprinkled with sesame seeds. This air-fried meal is diabetic-friendly, quick to prepare, and tasty.

Prep Time: 15 minutes

Cook Time: 10 minutes

Serves: 4

Ingredients:

- ➢ 1-pound beef sirloin, thinly sliced
- ➢ 1 red bell pepper, sliced
- ➢ 1 yellow bell pepper, sliced
- ➢ 1 cup broccoli florets

- ➢ 1/4 cup low-sodium teriyaki sauce

- ➢ 1 tablespoon sesame oil

- ➢ 1 teaspoon garlic, minced

- ➢ 1 teaspoon ginger, minced

- ➢ 2 tablespoons sesame seeds

- ➢ Salt and pepper to taste

Instructions:

1. Marinate the beef slices in teriyaki sauce, garlic, ginger, salt, and pepper in a bowl for at least 10 minutes.

2. Preheat the air fryer to 400°F (204°C).

3. Toss the marinated beef, bell peppers, and broccoli with sesame oil.

4. Place the mixture in the air fryer basket and cook for 10 minutes, shaking halfway through.

5. Garnish with sesame seeds before serving.

Nutritional Facts (Per serving):

- ❖ Calories: 270

- ❖ Carbohydrates: 12g

- ❖ Protein: 26g

- ❖ Fat: 14g

- ❖ Fiber: 2g

- ❖ Sugar: 6g

Delight in this Asian Teriyaki Beef, a dish combining the best nutrition and flavor. It's perfect for a quick yet delicious lunch that will keep you satisfied and your blood sugar in check.

CHAPTER 04: Weeknight Wonders: Easy Dinners

Recipe 31: Garlic Parmesan Chicken Thighs with Mushroom

Savor the delectable harmony of Garlic Parmesan Chicken Thighs accompanied by earthy mushrooms, all prepared in your air fryer. This dish elevates a simple dinner into a flavorful feast, perfect for managing a diabetic diet without compromising taste.

Prep Time: 10 minutes

Cook Time: 20 minutes

Serves: 4

Ingredients:

➢ 4 chicken thighs, bone-in, skin-on

- ➢ 1 cup mushrooms, sliced
- ➢ 1/4 cup grated Parmesan cheese
- ➢ 2 tablespoons olive oil
- ➢ 4 cloves garlic, minced
- ➢ 1 teaspoon Italian seasoning
- ➢ Salt and pepper to taste

Instructions:

1. In a bowl, combine olive oil, minced garlic, Italian seasoning, salt, and pepper. Rub this mixture all over the chicken thighs.
2. Preheat the air fryer to 380°F (193°C).
3. Arrange the skin side of the chicken thighs in the air fryer basket.
4. Cook for 10 minutes, then add the sliced mushrooms around the chicken.
5. Sprinkle Parmesan cheese over the chicken and continue cooking for another 10 minutes or until the chicken is fully cooked and the skin is crispy.
6. Serve hot, garnished with additional Parmesan if desired.

Nutritional Facts (Per serving):

- ❖ Calories: 310
- ❖ Carbohydrates: 3g
- ❖ Protein: 25g
- ❖ Fat: 22g
- ❖ Fiber: 0.5g
- ❖ Sugar: 1g

Relish this comforting Garlic Parmesan Chicken Thighs with Mushrooms, a dish sure to impress at any dinner table while fitting seamlessly into a diabetic-friendly meal plan.

Recipe 32: Blackened Salmon Fillet with Sweet Potato Wedges

Enjoy a meal as nutritious as it is delicious with Blackened Salmon Fillet paired with Sweet Potato Wedges. This air fryer recipe makes a perfect diabetic-friendly dinner, balancing rich flavors and essential nutrients.

Prep Time: 15 minutes

Cook Time: 20 minutes

Serves: 2

Ingredients:

- ➢ 2 salmon fillets, 6 oz each
- ➢ 2 tablespoons blackening seasoning
- ➢ 2 sweet potatoes, cut into wedges
- ➢ 1 tablespoon olive oil
- ➢ Salt and pepper to taste

Instructions:

1. Rub each salmon fillet with blackening seasoning.

2. Toss sweet potato wedges with olive oil, salt, and pepper.

3. Preheat the air fryer to 400°F (204°C).

4. Place sweet potato wedges in the air fryer for 10 minutes.

5. Add the seasoned salmon fillets to the air fryer with the sweet potatoes and cook for 10 minutes until the salmon is cooked and the potatoes are tender.

6. Serve immediately, garnished with fresh herbs if desired.

Nutritional Facts (Per serving):

❖ Calories: 420

❖ Carbohydrates: 30g

❖ Protein: 35g

❖ Fat: 18g

❖ Fiber: 4g

❖ Sugar: 6g

Delight in this Blackened Salmon Filet with Sweet Potato Wedges, a hearty and healthful dinner option that brings vibrant flavors and beneficial nutrients to your table. It's perfect for a satisfying evening meal.

Recipe 33: Baked Cod Fillet with Cherry Tomatoes and Butter

Dive into the light and flavorful Baked Cod Fillet with Cherry Tomatoes, enhanced with a touch of butter for richness. This simple air fryer dinner is diabetic-friendly, focusing on fresh ingredients and straightforward preparation for a delightful meal.

Prep Time: 5 minutes

Cook Time: 12 minutes

Serves: 2

Ingredients:

➢ 2 cod fillets, 6 oz each

➢ 1 cup cherry tomatoes, halved

➢ 2 tablespoons unsalted butter

➢ 1 lemon, sliced

- ➤ Salt and pepper to taste
- ➤ Fresh basil for garnish

Instructions:

1. Season the cod fillets with salt and pepper.

2. Place a few lemon slices on each fillet and top each with a tablespoon of butter.

3. Arrange the cherry tomatoes around the cod in the air fryer basket.

4. Preheat the air fryer to 400°F (204°C).

5. Cook for 12 minutes or until the cod is flaky and opaque and the tomatoes are soft.

6. Garnish with fresh basil before serving.

Nutritional Facts (Per serving):

- ❖ Calories: 280
- ❖ Carbohydrates: 6g
- ❖ Protein: 31g
- ❖ Fat: 14g
- ❖ Fiber: 1g
- ❖ Sugar: 3g

Relish this Baked Cod Fillet with Cherry Tomatoes. This dish promises a satisfying yet healthy dinner, perfectly suited for those managing diabetes or anyone looking for a nutritious meal.

Recipe 34: Traditional Tex-Mex Beef Enchiladas

Savor the bold flavors of Traditional Tex-Mex Beef Enchiladas, a hearty dish that transforms simple ingredients into a fiesta on your plate. This air fryer recipe offers a diabetic-friendly version without sacrificing the rich taste and satisfaction.

Prep Time: 20 minutes

Cook Time: 15 minutes

Serves: 4

Ingredients:

- ➤ 1 lb. lean ground beef
- ➤ 4 whole wheat tortillas
- ➤ 1 cup low-sodium enchilada sauce
- ➤ 1/2 cup shredded low-fat cheddar cheese

- ➢ 1 onion, diced
- ➢ 1 bell pepper, diced
- ➢ 2 cloves garlic, minced
- ➢ 1 teaspoon cumin
- ➢ Salt and pepper to taste
- ➢ Fresh cilantro, chopped for garnish

Instructions:

1. Brown the ground beef in a skillet with onions, bell pepper, garlic, cumin, salt, and pepper. Drain any excess fat.

2. Warm tortillas slightly to make them pliable. Divide the beef mixture among the tortillas, roll them up tightly, and place them seam-side down in the air fryer basket.

3. Spoon enchilada sauce over the rolled tortillas and sprinkle with cheese.

4. Cook in the air fryer at 360°F (182°C) for 15 minutes or until the cheese is melted and bubbly.

5. Garnish with fresh cilantro before serving.

Nutritional Facts (Per serving):

- ❖ Calories: 350
- ❖ Fat: 15g
- ❖ Carbohydrates: 28g
- ❖ Fiber: 5g
- ❖ Protein: 27g
- ❖ Sugar: 5g

Enjoy these delicious Traditional Tex-Mex Beef Enchiladas, a comforting meal that brings warmth and joy to your dinner table. They are perfect for a fulfilling evening while effectively managing your dietary needs.

Recipe 35: Stir-Fried Minced Pork with Basil

Experience the aromatic flavors of Stir-Fried Minced Pork with Basil, a classic Thai dish that's quick and simple to prepare in your air fryer. This diabetic-friendly dinner bursts with spicy, sweet, and savory notes, ideal for a satisfying weeknight meal.

Prep Time: 10 minutes

Cook Time: 8 minutes

Serves: 2

Ingredients:

- ➤ 1 lb. minced pork
- ➤ 1 cup fresh basil leaves
- ➤ 2 cloves garlic, minced
- ➤ 2 tablespoons soy sauce (low sodium)
- ➤ 1 tablespoon fish sauce

- ➤ 1 teaspoon sugar substitute

- ➤ 1 small chili, sliced

- ➤ 1 tablespoon vegetable oil

Instructions:

1. Preheat the air fryer to 350°F (177°C).

2. Mix the minced pork with garlic, soy sauce, fish sauce, sugar substitute, and chili.

3. Heat the vegetable oil over medium heat, then add the pork mixture. Cook until the pork is browned.

4. Transfer the cooked pork to the air fryer basket and cook for 8 minutes, stirring halfway through.

5. Stir in the fresh basil leaves just before serving to keep them vibrant and fresh.

Nutritional Facts (Per serving):

- ❖ Calories: 430

- ❖ Carbohydrates: 4g

- ❖ Protein: 25g

- ❖ Fat: 34g

- ❖ Fiber: 1g

- ❖ Sugar: 1g

Relish the bold and refreshing flavors of Stir-Fried Minced Pork with Basil, a perfect dish to uplift your spirits and satisfy your cravings while adhering to a diabetic-friendly diet.

Recipe 36: Herb-Crusted Rack of Lamb

Elevate your dinner with this Herb-Crusted Rack of Lamb, a luxurious dish that's simple to make in your air fryer. This diabetic-friendly recipe combines aromatic herbs with tender lamb for a truly gourmet experience at home.

Prep Time: 15 minutes

Cook Time: 22 minutes

Serves: 2

Ingredients:

- 1 rack of lamb (about 8 ribs)
- 2 tablespoons Dijon mustard
- 1/4 cup fresh bread crumbs
- 2 tablespoons fresh rosemary, chopped
- 2 tablespoons fresh thyme, chopped

- ➤ 2 cloves garlic, minced

- ➤ Salt and pepper to taste

- ➤ 1 tablespoon olive oil

Instructions:

1. Preheat the air fryer to 400°F (204°C).

2. Season the rack of lamb with salt and pepper.

3. Rub the lamb with Dijon mustard.

4. Mix bread crumbs, rosemary, thyme, garlic, and olive oil in a bowl. Press this herb mixture onto the mustard-coated lamb.

5. Place the lamb in the air fryer and cook for 22 minutes for medium-rare, or adjust the time to reach your preferred doneness.

6. Let the lamb rest for 5 minutes before slicing between the ribs and serving.

Nutritional Facts (Per serving):

- ❖ Calories: 580

- ❖ Carbohydrates: 8g

- ❖ Protein: 45g

- ❖ Fat: 40g

- ❖ Fiber: 1g

- ❖ Sugar: 1g

Savor the rich flavors and succulent texture of this Herb-Crusted Rack of Lamb, a dish that will impress any guest and make your evening meal a little more special.

Recipe 37: Roasted BBQ Duck Breast with Potato Wedge Fries

Delight in the rich flavors of Roasted BBQ Duck Breast and crispy potato wedge fries, all made easily in your air fryer. This diabetic-friendly dinner melds succulent duck with the homely comfort of potatoes for a balanced, satisfying meal.

Prep Time: 15 minutes

Cook Time: 25 minutes

Serves: 2

Ingredients:

- ➢ 2 duck breasts
- ➢ 2 tablespoons BBQ sauce (sugar-free)
- ➢ 4 large potatoes, cut into wedges
- ➢ 1 tablespoon olive oil

- ➢ Salt and pepper to taste
- ➢ Fresh parsley, chopped (for garnish)

Instructions:

1. Score the duck breast skin in a crisscross pattern—season both sides with salt and pepper.

2. Brush the duck breasts with BBQ sauce.

3. Toss the potato wedges with olive oil and a pinch of salt.

4. Preheat the air fryer to 360°F (182°C).

5. Place the duck breasts skin side down in the air fryer basket and cook for 10 minutes.

6. Add the potato wedges around the duck, then cook everything for 15 minutes, turning the duck once and shaking the potatoes halfway through.

7. Garnish with fresh parsley before serving.

Nutritional Facts (Per serving):

- ❖ Calories: 520
- ❖ Carbohydrates: 38g
- ❖ Protein: 27g
- ❖ Fat: 27g
- ❖ Fiber: 5g
- ❖ Sugar: 3g

Relax and enjoy this gourmet Roasted BBQ Duck Breast meal with Potato Wedge Fries. This dish brings restaurant-quality dining into the comfort of your home, perfect for a cozy and delicious diabetic-friendly dinner.

Recipe 38: Glazed Chicken Thighs with Sesame Seeds

Indulge in the savory sweetness of Glazed Chicken Thighs with Sesame Seeds, a delightful dish that combines juicy chicken with a diabetic-friendly glaze. This air fryer recipe delivers a crispy finish with a burst of flavor, perfect for an enjoyable dinner.

Prep Time: 10 minutes

Cook Time: 20 minutes

Serves: 4

Ingredients:

➢ 4 chicken thighs, bone-in, skin-on

➢ 2 tablespoons soy sauce (low sodium)

➢ 2 tablespoons honey substitute

➢ 1 tablespoon sesame oil

- ➤ 1 teaspoon garlic powder
- ➤ 1 tablespoon sesame seeds
- ➤ Salt and pepper to taste

Instructions:

1. Mix soy sauce, honey substitute, sesame oil, and garlic powder in a small bowl to make the glaze.

2. Season the chicken thighs with salt and pepper, then brush them with the glaze.

3. Preheat the air fryer to 380°F (193°C).

4. Place the chicken thighs skin side up in the air fryer basket and cook for 20 minutes until the chicken is cooked through and the skin is crispy.

5. Sprinkle sesame seeds over the chicken thighs in the last 5 minutes of cooking.

6. Serve hot.

Nutritional Facts (Per serving):

- ❖ Calories: 310
- ❖ Carbohydrates: 3g
- ❖ Protein: 24g
- ❖ Fat: 22g
- ❖ Fiber: 0g
- ❖ Sugar: 1g

Enjoy these Glazed Chicken Thighs with Sesame Seeds, a simple yet elegant meal that will satisfy your taste buds while keeping health considerations in check. Perfect for a family dinner or a special occasion.

Recipe 39: Wild Rabbit Cooked with Lemon

Dive into the rustic flavors of Wild Rabbit Cooked with Lemon, a unique dish that highlights the subtle gameness of rabbit paired with bright citrus notes. This air fryer recipe provides a diabetic-friendly dinner option that's as nutritious as delicious.

Prep Time: 15 minutes

Cook Time: 30 minutes

Serves: 2

Ingredients:

➤ 1 whole wild rabbit, cleaned and cut into pieces

➤ 2 lemons, one juiced and one sliced

➤ 2 tablespoons olive oil

➤ 4 garlic cloves, minced

➤ 1 teaspoon rosemary

➤ Salt and pepper to taste

Instructions:

1. Marinate the rabbit pieces in olive oil, lemon juice, garlic, rosemary, salt, and pepper in the refrigerator for at least 1 hour.

2. Preheat the air fryer to 350°F (177°C).

3. Place the rabbit pieces in the air fryer basket and arrange lemon slices around them.

4. Cook for 30 minutes until the rabbit is tender and fully cooked, turning the pieces halfway through cooking.

5. Serve hot, garnished with fresh herbs if desired.

Nutritional Facts (Per serving):

❖ Calories: 380

❖ Carbohydrates: 5g

❖ Protein: 54g

❖ Fat: 16g

❖ Fiber: 1g

❖ Sugar: 1g

Savor the delightful combination of wild rabbit with lemon, a meal that's both heartily satisfying and suitable for a healthy diet. Perfect for those who appreciate game meat with a twist of fresh flavors.

Recipe 40: Cajun Blackened Catfish with French Fries

Dive into the bold flavors of the South with Cajun Blackened Catfish paired with crispy French fries. This air fryer meal brings the zest and spice of Cajun seasoning in a diabetic-friendly format, offering a delicious and satisfying dinner option.

Prep Time: 10 minutes

Cook Time: 20 minutes

Serves: 2

Ingredients:

➢ 2 catfish fillets

➢ 2 tablespoons Cajun seasoning

➢ 2 large potatoes, cut into fries

➢ 1 tablespoon olive oil

> ➢ Salt to taste

Instructions:

1. Coat the catfish fillets evenly with Cajun seasoning.

2. Toss the potato fries with olive oil and a pinch of salt.

3. Preheat the air fryer to 400°F (204°C).

4. Cook the fries in the air fryer for 10 minutes, then add the catfish fillets.

5. Cook everything together for 10 minutes or until the catfish is opaque and flakes easily with a fork.

6. Serve immediately.

Nutritional Facts (Per serving):

- ❖ Calories: 390

- ❖ Carbohydrates: 38g

- ❖ Protein: 35g

- ❖ Fat: 12g

- ❖ Fiber: 3g

- ❖ Sugar: 2g

Enjoy this Cajun Blackened Catfish with French fries, a lively and flavorful dish that brings a taste of Louisiana straight to your dinner table while keeping your health in check. Perfect for a delicious, fuss-free meal.

Recipe 41: Grilled Spicy Chicken Wings with Ketchup

Ignite your taste buds with Grilled Spicy Chicken Wings accompanied by ketchup. This air fryer recipe delivers the perfect blend of heat and sweetness, offering a diabetic-friendly dinner that will satisfy your craving for something spicy.

Prep Time: 15 minutes

Cook Time: 25 minutes

Serves: 2

Ingredients:

- ➤ 1-pound chicken wings
- ➤ 2 tablespoons hot sauce
- ➤ 1 tablespoon olive oil
- ➤ 1 teaspoon garlic powder

- ➢ 1 teaspoon smoked paprika
- ➢ Salt and pepper to taste
- ➢ Sugar-free ketchup for dipping

Instructions:

1. Mix hot sauce, olive oil, garlic powder, smoked paprika, salt, and pepper in a bowl. Toss the chicken wings in the mixture until well coated.

2. Preheat the air fryer to 360°F (182°C).

3. Arrange the wings in the air fryer basket. Cook for 25 minutes, turning halfway through, until crispy and cooked through.

4. Serve hot with sugar-free ketchup for dipping.

Nutritional Facts (Per serving):

- ❖ Calories: 440
- ❖ Carbohydrates: 5g
- ❖ Protein: 35g
- ❖ Fat: 32g
- ❖ Fiber: 1g
- ❖ Sugar: 1g

Enjoy these Grilled Spicy Chicken Wings, a fiery and delightful treat that pairs perfectly with the coolness of sugar-free ketchup, making your dinner both enjoyable and health-conscious.

Recipe 42: Roasted Spicy Glazed Pork Roll

Savor the tantalizing flavors of Roasted Spicy Glazed Pork Roll with rich tomato sauce, fried potatoes, and fresh herbs. This air-fried masterpiece offers a diabetic-friendly dinner that's as hearty as it is delicious.

Prep Time: 20 minutes

Cook Time: 40 minutes

Serves: 4

Ingredients:

- ➢ 1 pork tenderloin (about 1.5 pounds)
- ➢ 2 tablespoons olive oil
- ➢ 2 tablespoons spicy glaze (sugar-free BBQ sauce mixed with chili flakes)
- ➢ 4 medium potatoes, sliced
- ➢ 1 cup tomato sauce (low sugar)

- ➢ 1 tablespoon mixed herbs (rosemary, thyme, basil)
- ➢ Salt and pepper to taste

Instructions:

1. Rub the pork tenderloin with salt, pepper, and 1 tablespoon olive oil. Then, coat it with a spicy glaze.

2. Preheat the air fryer to 350°F (177°C).

3. Cook the pork in the air fryer for 30 minutes.

4. Meanwhile, toss the potato slices with the remaining olive oil, salt, and herbs.

5. After 30 minutes, add the potatoes to the air fryer around the pork. Continue cooking for 10 minutes or until the pork is cooked through and the potatoes are crispy.

6. Warm the tomato sauce separately.

7. Slice the pork and serve with fried potatoes and warm tomato sauce.

Nutritional Facts (Per serving):

- ❖ Calories: 390
- ❖ Carbohydrates: 38g
- ❖ Protein: 34g
- ❖ Fat: 12g
- ❖ Fiber: 5g
- ❖ Sugar: 6g

Indulge in this Roasted Spicy Glazed Pork Roll, a flavorful dinner that perfectly balances spice with savory. The crunch of fried potatoes and the freshness of herbs complement the dish.

Recipe 43: Grilled Gnocchi Steak and Red Pepper Skewers

Elevate your dining experience with Grilled Gnocchi Steak and Red Pepper Skewers, a creative combination that blends hearty textures and flavors. This diabetic-friendly air fryer recipe turns simple ingredients into a visually stunning and delicious meal.

Prep Time: 15 minutes

Cook Time: 10 minutes

Serves: 4

Ingredients:

- ➤ 1-pound sirloin steak, cut into cubes
- ➤ 1-pound gnocchi, pre-cooked
- ➤ 2 red bell peppers, cut into pieces
- ➤ 2 tablespoons olive oil

- ➢ 1 teaspoon garlic powder

- ➢ Salt and pepper to taste

- ➢ Fresh parsley, chopped for garnish

Instructions:

1. Toss the steak cubes and gnocchi with olive oil, garlic powder, salt, and pepper.

2. Thread the steak, gnocchi, and red pepper pieces alternately onto skewers.

3. Preheat the air fryer to 400°F (204°C).

4. Place the skewers in the air fryer basket and cook for 10 minutes, turning halfway through, until the steak is cooked to your desired doneness and the gnocchi is golden.

5. Garnish with chopped parsley before serving.

Nutritional Facts (Per serving):

- ❖ Calories: 490

- ❖ Carbohydrates: 47g

- ❖ Protein: 29g

- ❖ Fat: 21g

- ❖ Fiber: 3g

- ❖ Sugar: 3g

Enjoy these Grilled Gnocchi Steak and Red Pepper Skewers, a delightful dish that combines the best of grilled meats and comforting gnocchi. They are perfect for a special dinner that is both satisfying and suitable for a diabetic diet.

Recipe 44: Baked Salmon Stuffed with Spinach and Cheese

Delight in the sumptuous flavors of Baked Salmon Stuffed with Spinach, Cheese, and Lemon—a gourmet creation that's surprisingly simple to prepare in your air fryer. This dish brings flavor to each bite, perfect for a diabetic-friendly dinner.

Prep Time: 20 minutes

Cook Time: 15 minutes

Serves: 2

Ingredients:

- ➢ 2 salmon fillets (6 oz each)
- ➢ 1 cup fresh spinach, chopped
- ➢ 1/2 cup low-fat cream cheese
- ➢ 1 lemon, zest and juice

- ➢ 2 cloves garlic, minced
- ➢ Salt and pepper to taste
- ➢ Olive oil

Instructions:

1. Preheat the air fryer to 375°F (190°C).

2. Mix the spinach, cream cheese, lemon zest, lemon juice, and garlic in a bowl. Season with salt and pepper.

3. Cut a slit in each salmon fillet to create a pocket. Stuff the spinach and cheese mixture into the pockets.

4. Lightly brush the outside of the salmon with olive oil.

5. Place the stuffed salmon in the air fryer basket.

6. Cook for 15 minutes or until the salmon is cooked and the stuffing is hot.

7. Serve immediately, drizzled with extra lemon juice if desired.

Nutritional Facts (Per serving):

- ❖ Calories: 420
- ❖ Carbohydrates: 5g
- ❖ Protein: 35g
- ❖ Fat: 28g
- ❖ Fiber: 1g
- ❖ Sugar: 2g

Enjoy this Baked Salmon Stuffed with Spinach and Cheese, an elegant yet easy dish that brings sophisticated flavors to your dinner table, perfect for keeping your meal healthy and your palate satisfied.

Recipe 45: Roasted Whole Chicken with Rosemary

Savor the classic comfort of Roasted Whole Chicken with Rosemary, an effortless yet elegant dinner option cooked in your air fryer. This diabetic-friendly dish promises a flavorful and nutritious meal for any occasion.

Prep Time: 10 minutes

Cook Time: 60 minutes

Serves: 4

Ingredients:

- ➢ 1 whole chicken (about 4 lbs.)
- ➢ 2 tablespoons olive oil
- ➢ 3 sprigs fresh rosemary
- ➢ 1 lemon, halved
- ➢ 4 cloves garlic, minced

➤ Salt and pepper to taste

Instructions:

1. Rub the chicken with olive oil and season generously with salt, pepper, and minced garlic.

2. Stuff the cavity with rosemary sprigs and lemon halves.

3. Preheat the air fryer to 360°F (182°C).

4. Place the chicken in the air fryer basket, breast side down. Cook for 30 minutes.

5. Flip the chicken breast and cook for 30 minutes until the internal temperature reaches 165°F (74°C).

6. Let the chicken rest for 10 minutes before carving.

Nutritional Facts (Per serving):

❖ Calories: 410

❖ Carbohydrates: 1g

❖ Protein: 35g

❖ Fat: 30g

❖ Fiber: 0g

❖ Sugar: 0g

Indulge in this Roasted Whole Chicken with Rosemary, a meal that combines simplicity and sophisticated flavors. It provides a hearty, satisfying dinner perfectly aligned with a health-conscious lifestyle.

CHAPTER 05: Guilt-Free Pleasures: Desserts and Snacks

Recipe 46: Peach Cobbler with Pastry Crust

Enjoy the sweet and comforting taste of Peach Cobbler with Pastry Crust, a delightful dessert that's made easy in your air fryer. This version offers a diabetic-friendly twist, allowing you to indulge without worry.

Prep Time: 15 minutes

Cook Time: 20 minutes

Serves: 4

Ingredients:

➤ 4 large peaches, sliced

➤ 1 cup whole wheat pastry flour

- ➢ 1/4 cup sugar substitute

- ➢ 1/2 teaspoon cinnamon

- ➢ 1/4 cup unsalted butter, chilled and diced

- ➢ 1/4 cup cold water

- ➢ Pinch of salt

Instructions:

1. Mix the peaches with cinnamon and half of the sugar substitute in a bowl.

2. Combine pastry flour, the remaining sugar substitute, and salt in another bowl. Work the butter into the flour mixture until crumbly. Gradually add cold water to form a dough.

3. Place the peach mixture in the air fryer basket. Top with flattened pieces of dough.

4. Preheat the air fryer to 350°F (177°C).

5. Cook for 20 minutes or until the crust is golden and the peaches are bubbly.

6. Let cool slightly before serving.

Nutritional Facts (Per serving):

- ❖ Calories: 250
- ❖ Carbohydrates: 38g
- ❖ Protein: 4g
- ❖ Fat: 10g
- ❖ Fiber: 5g
- ❖ Sugar: 15g

This Peach Cobbler with Pastry Crust is the perfect treat to satisfy your sweet tooth. It offers a classic dessert experience that's both tasty and tailored for a diabetic diet. Enjoy it warm for a cozy end to any meal.

Recipe 47: Banana Nut Bread

Indulge in the comforting taste of Banana Nut Bread, now lighter and suited for a diabetic diet, thanks to your air fryer. This wholesome treat blends ripe bananas and crunchy nuts for a satisfying snack or dessert.

Prep Time: 15 minutes

Cook Time: 25 minutes

Serves: 2

Ingredients:

- ➢ 1 ripe banana, mashed
- ➢ 1 cup whole wheat flour
- ➢ 1/3 cup sugar substitute
- ➢ 1/2 teaspoon baking soda
- ➢ 1/4 cup chopped walnuts

- ➤ 1 egg
- ➤ 1/4 cup unsweetened almond milk
- ➤ 1/2 teaspoon vanilla extract
- ➤ Pinch of salt

Instructions:

1. Combine mashed banana, egg, almond milk, and vanilla extract in a bowl.
2. Mix whole wheat flour, sugar substitute, baking soda, and salt in another bowl.
3. Fold the dry ingredients into the wet ingredients until they are combined. Stir in walnuts.
4. Pour the batter into a greased air fryer-safe baking pan.
5. Preheat the air fryer to 320°F (160°C).
6. Cook for 25 minutes or until a toothpick inserted into the center comes clean.
7. Allow to cool before slicing and serving.

Nutritional Facts (Per serving):

- ❖ Calories: 280
- ❖ Carbohydrates: 44g
- ❖ Protein: 9g
- ❖ Fat: 10g
- ❖ Fiber: 6g
- ❖ Sugar: 12g

Enjoy this Banana Nut Bread, a delightful, nourishing, and delicious treat. It's perfect for a quick breakfast or a cozy afternoon snack and is tailored to fit a health-conscious lifestyle.

Recipe 48: Mixed Berry Cobbler

Delight in the vibrant flavors of a Mixed Berry Cobbler, perfectly sweetened and ready in minutes with your air fryer. This diabetic-friendly dessert layers juicy berries under a light, fluffy topping, offering a guilt-free treat to satisfy any sweet tooth.

Prep Time: 10 minutes

Cook Time: 15 minutes

Serves: 4

Ingredients:

- ➤ 2 cups mixed berries (fresh or frozen)
- ➤ 1 cup almond flour
- ➤ 1/4 cup sugar substitute
- ➤ 1/4 cup unsalted butter, melted
- ➤ 1 teaspoon vanilla extract

- ➤ 1/2 teaspoon baking powder
- ➤ Pinch of salt

Instructions:

1. Mix berries with a tablespoon of sugar substitute and vanilla extract in a bowl. Place in an air fryer-safe dish.

2. Combine almond flour, remaining sugar substitute, baking powder, salt, and melted butter until crumbly in another bowl.

3. Sprinkle the crumbly mixture over the berries.

4. Cook in the air fryer at 350°F (177°C) for 15 minutes or until the topping is golden and the berries are bubbling.

5. Let cool slightly before serving.

Nutritional Facts (Per serving):

- ❖ Calories: 240
- ❖ Carbohydrates: 18g
- ❖ Protein: 5g
- ❖ Fat: 18g
- ❖ Fiber: 4g
- ❖ Sugar: 8g

Enjoy this delicious Mixed Berry Cobbler, a simple and delightful way to end your meal, or enjoy a snack that feels indulgent while fitting seamlessly into a diabetic diet.

Recipe 49: British Scones with Cream Cheese

Indulge in the quintessentially British experience with these delightful Scones, served with cream cheese and strawberry jam. This diabetic-friendly version, made in your air fryer, brings a touch of elegance to your tea time while keeping health in mind.

Prep Time: 15 minutes

Cook Time: 15 minutes

Serves: 4

Ingredients:

- ➢ 2 cups almond flour
- ➢ 1/3 cup sugar substitute
- ➢ 1/2 cup heavy cream
- ➢ 1 large egg
- ➢ 2 teaspoons baking powder

- ➢ 1 teaspoon vanilla extract
- ➢ Pinch of salt
- ➢ 1/4 cup cream cheese
- ➢ 1/4 cup sugar-free strawberry jam

Instructions:

1. Mix almond flour, sugar substitute, baking powder, and salt in a bowl.
2. whisk together cream, egg, and vanilla extract in another bowl.
3. Combine wet and dry ingredients until a dough form.
4. Form into small rounds and place on a greased air fryer basket.
5. Cook in the air fryer at 320°F (160°C) for 15 minutes or until golden.
6. Serve warm with cream cheese and strawberry jam.

Nutritional Facts (Per serving):

- ❖ Calories: 385
- ❖ Carbohydrates: 18g
- ❖ Protein: 10g
- ❖ Fat: 32g
- ❖ Fiber: 4g
- ❖ Sugar: 2g

Savor these British Scones, a delightful and nutritious treat that perfectly combines traditional flavors with a healthier twist, ideal for enjoying a special snack or dessert any time of day.

Recipe 50: Clotted Cream Rice Pudding

Experience the creamy, comforting delight of Clotted Cream Rice Pudding, a luxurious dessert that's surprisingly simple to prepare in your air fryer. This diabetic-friendly version allows you to enjoy a classic treat without sugar overload.

Prep Time: 5 minutes

Cook Time: 25 minutes

Serves: 4

Ingredients:

- ➢ 1 cup Arborio rice
- ➢ 3 cups almond milk
- ➢ 1/4 cup sugar substitute
- ➢ 1/2 cup clotted cream
- ➢ 1 teaspoon vanilla extract

- ➢ Pinch of cinnamon
- ➢ Fresh berries for garnish

Instructions:

1. Combine rice, almond milk, and sugar substitute in the air fryer-safe dish. Stir well.

2. Cook in the air fryer at 320°F (160°C) for 25 minutes, stirring halfway through until rice is tender and creamy.

3. Stir in clotted cream and vanilla extract after cooking.

4. Serve warm, sprinkled with cinnamon, and topped with fresh berries.

Nutritional Facts (Per serving):

- ❖ Calories: 320
- ❖ Carbohydrates: 40g
- ❖ Protein: 5g
- ❖ Fat: 15g
- ❖ Fiber: 1g
- ❖ Sugar: 1g

Enjoy this rich and creamy Clotted Cream Rice Pudding, a delightful way to indulge in a classic dessert that satisfies your sweet cravings while being kind to your diabetic dietary needs. Perfect for a cozy evening treat or a festive occasion.

Recipe 51: Fried Cinnamon Sugar Donut Holes

Delve into the delightful crunch of Fried Cinnamon Sugar Donut Holes, a treat made healthier in your air fryer. This diabetic-friendly recipe offers all the joy of a classic donut without worry, perfect for satisfying those sweet cravings.

Prep Time: 10 minutes

Cook Time: 8 minutes

Serves: 4

Ingredients:

- 1 cup almond flour
- 1/4 cup coconut flour
- 1/4 cup sugar substitute
- 2 teaspoons baking powder
- 1 teaspoon cinnamon

- 1 egg
- 1/4 cup unsweetened almond milk
- 1 teaspoon vanilla extract
- Cooking spray

For coating:

- 2 tablespoons melted butter
- 1/4 cup sugar substitute
- 1 teaspoon cinnamon

Instructions:

1. Mix almond flour, coconut flour, sugar substitute, baking powder, and cinnamon in a bowl.

2. Stir in egg, almond milk, and vanilla extract until well combined.

3. Form the mixture into small balls.

4. Preheat the air fryer to 350°F (177°C) and lightly spray the basket with cooking spray.

5. Place the donut holes in the basket and cook for 8 minutes, shaking halfway through.

6. Mix additional sugar substitute and cinnamon in a bowl. Brush cooked donut holes with melted butter and roll in the cinnamon sugar mixture.

7. Serve warm.

Nutritional Facts (Per serving):

- ❖ Calories: 200
- ❖ Carbohydrates: 10g
- ❖ Protein: 6g
- ❖ Fat: 16g
- ❖ Fiber: 3g
- ❖ Sugar: 1g

Relish these Fried Cinnamon Sugar Donut Holes, a perfect little treat with immense flavor. These donut holes are ideal for a cozy morning or as a delightful snack, making indulgence easy and health-conscious.

Recipe 52: Pistachio Baklava

Discover the exquisite layers of Pistachio Baklava, a decadent dessert made healthier in your air fryer. This diabetic-friendly treat combines thin pastry with rich pistachios and a hint of sweetness, offering an indulgent experience without the excess sugar.

Prep Time: 20 minutes

Cook Time: 15 minutes

Serves: 2

Ingredients:

➤ 4 sheets of phyllo dough

➤ 1/2 cup chopped pistachios

➤ 2 tablespoons unsalted butter, melted

➤ 2 tablespoons sugar substitute

➤ 1/2 teaspoon ground cinnamon

For the syrup:

- 1/4 cup water

- 2 tablespoons sugar substitute

- 1/4 teaspoon lemon juice

- 1/4 teaspoon vanilla extract

Instructions:

1. Brush each phyllo sheet with melted butter and sprinkle a pistachio, sugar substitute, and cinnamon layer. Stack the sheets.

2. Cut into triangles or squares and place in a greased air fryer basket.

3. Preheat the air fryer to 350°F (177°C).

4. Cook for 15 minutes or until golden brown.

5. make the syrup by combining water, sugar substitute, lemon juice, and vanilla in a saucepan. Simmer until thickened.

6. Drizzle syrup over the hot baklava after it's cooked.

7. Allow to cool before serving.

Nutritional Facts (Per serving):

- Calories: 310
- Fat: 24g

- Carbohydrates: 18g
- Fiber: 3g

- Protein: 6g
- Sugar: 5g

Enjoy this Pistachio Baklava, a delightfully crispy and nutty treat that perfectly caps off any meal or serves as a splendid afternoon snack while fitting into a diabetic diet.

Recipe 53: Peanut Butter Cookies

Enjoy the timeless taste of Peanut Butter Cookies, now made in your air fryer for a healthier twist. This diabetic-friendly version keeps peanut butter's creamy goodness in a delightfully chewy treat that's easy and quick to prepare.

Prep Time: 10 minutes

Cook Time: 8 minutes

Serves: 4

Ingredients:

- 1 cup natural peanut butter
- 1/3 cup sugar substitute
- 1 egg
- 1 teaspoon vanilla extract

Instructions:

1. Mix all ingredients in a bowl until well combined.

2. Place the dough into 1-inch balls on a parchment-lined air fryer basket, flattening each slightly.

3. Preheat the air fryer to 320°F (160°C).

4. Cook for 8 minutes or until the cookies are lightly browned and firm to the touch.

5. Allow the cookies to cool on a rack before serving.

Nutritional Facts (Per serving):

- ❖ Calories: 280
- ❖ Carbohydrates: 9g
- ❖ Protein: 10g
- ❖ Fat: 24g
- ❖ Fiber: 3g
- ❖ Sugar: 4g

These Peanut Butter Cookies are a perfect way to satisfy your dessert cravings. They offer a classic flavor with a healthy makeover, ideal for sharing with friends and family. Enjoy them as a snack or a sweet end to your meal.

Recipe 54: Spiced Pumpkin Muffins

Welcome the flavors of fall any time of year with these Spiced Pumpkin Muffins, baked to perfection in your air fryer. These muffins are delicious and diabetic-friendly, making them an excellent treat for anyone looking to indulge healthily.

Prep Time: 10 minutes

Cook Time: 15 minutes

Serves: 6

Ingredients:

- ➢ 1 cup almond flour
- ➢ 1/2 cup canned pumpkin puree
- ➢ 1/4 cup sugar substitute
- ➢ 2 eggs
- ➢ 1 teaspoon baking powder

- ➢ 1 teaspoon cinnamon
- ➢ 1/2 teaspoon nutmeg
- ➢ 1/4 teaspoon ground cloves
- ➢ 1/4 teaspoon salt

Instructions:

1. Combine pumpkin puree, sugar substitute, eggs, and spices in a mixing bowl until smooth.
2. Mix in almond flour, baking powder, and salt until just combined.
3. Spoon batter into a silicone muffin mold to fit in the air fryer basket.
4. Preheat the air fryer to 350°F (177°C).
5. Cook muffins for 15 minutes or until a toothpick inserted into the center comes clean.
6. Allow to cool slightly before serving.

Nutritional Facts (Per serving):

- ❖ Calories: 180
- ❖ Carbohydrates: 8g
- ❖ Protein: 6g
- ❖ Fat: 14g
- ❖ Fiber: 3g
- ❖ Sugar: 2g

Enjoy these warm, spiced pumpkin muffins—a comforting, tasty snack that brings the essence of autumn to your table without compromising your dietary needs. Perfect with a cup of tea or as a quick breakfast option!

Recipe 55: Coconut Macaroons

Experience the divine simplicity of Coconut Macaroons, perfectly crispy on the outside and delightfully chewy inside. These diabetic-friendly treats provide a guilt-free way to indulge in your sweet tooth.

Prep Time: 10 minutes

Cook Time: 10 minutes

Serves: 3

Ingredients:

- ➢ 1 1/2 cups unsweetened shredded coconut
- ➢ 1/4 cup sugar substitute
- ➢ 2 large egg whites
- ➢ 1 teaspoon vanilla extract
- ➢ Pinch of salt

Instructions:

1. Combine shredded coconut, sugar substitute, and salt in a mixing bowl.

2. Stir in egg whites and vanilla extract until well blended.

3. Place the mixture into small balls on a parchment-lined air fryer basket.

4. Preheat the air fryer to 320°F (160°C).

5. Cook for 10 minutes or until the macaroons are golden and firm to the touch.

6. Let cool before serving to allow them to firm up further.

Nutritional Facts (Per serving):

❖ Calories: 210

❖ Carbohydrates: 8g

❖ Protein: 3g

❖ Fat: 18g

❖ Fiber: 5g

❖ Sugar: 3g

Enjoy these Coconut Macaroons, a delightful concoction that combines the tropical zest of coconut with the ease of air frying, creating a perfect treat to enjoy after dinner or as a sweet snack.

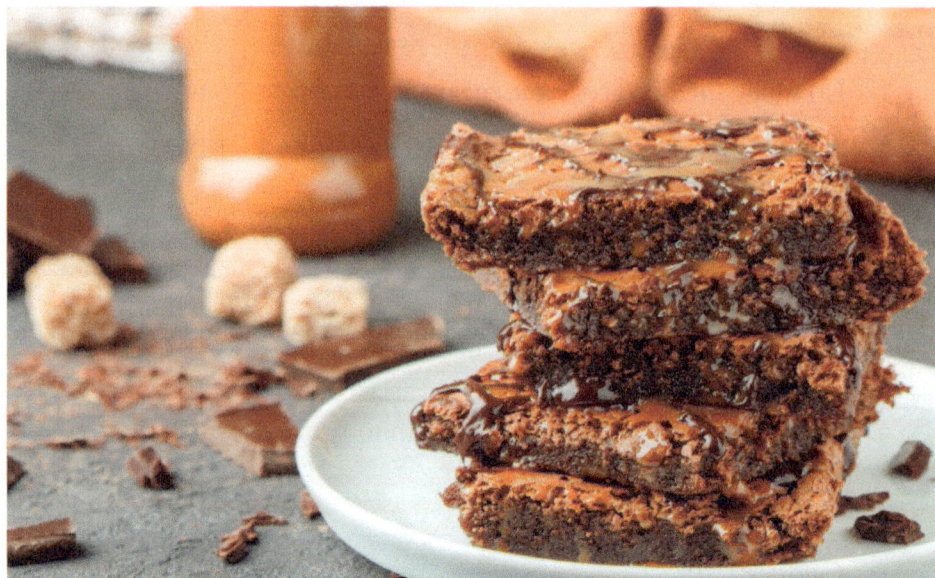

Recipe 56: Salted Caramel Brownies

Indulge in the irresistible blend of sweet and savory with Salted Caramel Brownies, perfectly crafted in your air fryer. These diabetic-friendly brownies are a decadent treat, offering the rich taste of caramel with a hint of sea salt.

Prep Time: 15 minutes

Cook Time: 20 minutes

Serves: 3

Ingredients:

- 1/2 cup almond flour
- 1/4 cup cocoa powder
- 1/4 cup sugar substitute
- 1/4 teaspoon baking powder
- 1/4 teaspoon sea salt
- 2 tablespoons unsalted butter, melted

- ➤ 1 large egg
- ➤ 1 teaspoon vanilla extract
- ➤ 2 tablespoons sugar-free caramel sauce

Instructions:

1. Mix almond flour, cocoa powder, sugar substitute, baking powder, and sea salt in a bowl.

2. Stir in melted butter, egg, and vanilla extract until well combined.

3. Pour the batter into a greased air fryer-safe baking dish.

4. Drizzle caramel sauce over the top and swirl into the batter with a toothpick.

5. Preheat the air fryer to 350°F (177°C).

6. Cook for 20 minutes or until a toothpick inserted into the center is clean.

7. Let cool before slicing into pieces.

Nutritional Facts (Per serving):

- ❖ Calories: 215
- ❖ Carbohydrates: 10g
- ❖ Protein: 6g
- ❖ Fat: 18g
- ❖ Fiber: 3g
- ❖ Sugar: 1g

Savor these Salted Caramel Brownies, a perfect combination of indulgence and health-conscious choices. They are an ideal treat for those looking to satisfy their dessert cravings while managing dietary restrictions.

Recipe 57: Fried Apple Fritter Donut with Cinnamon

Enjoy the delightful crunch of Fried Apple Fritter Donuts infused with cinnamon and made healthier in your air fryer. This diabetic-friendly recipe captures the essence of a classic treat, allowing you to indulge without the guilt.

Prep Time: 15 minutes

Cook Time: 8 minutes

Serves: 3

Ingredients:

➢ 1 large apple, peeled and diced

➢ 1 cup almond flour

➢ 1/4 cup sugar substitute

➢ 1 teaspoon cinnamon

➢ 1/2 teaspoon baking powder

- ➢ 1 egg
- ➢ 1/4 cup unsweetened almond milk
- ➢ Cooking spray

Instructions:

1. Combine almond flour, sugar substitute, cinnamon, and baking powder in a mixing bowl.

2. Stir in egg and almond milk to form a batter. Fold in diced apples.

3. Preheat the air fryer to 350°F (177°C).

4. Form the batter into small patties and place in a greased air fryer basket.

5. Cook for 8 minutes, flipping halfway through, until golden and cooked through.

6. Let cool slightly before serving.

Nutritional Facts (Per serving):

- ❖ Calories: 230
- ❖ Carbohydrates: 15g
- ❖ Protein: 9g
- ❖ Fat: 16g
- ❖ Fiber: 4g
- ❖ Sugar: 5g

Dive into these warm, crispy Fried Apple Fritter Donuts, a heavenly combination of sweet apples and cinnamon that brings comfort and joy with every bite. Perfect for a cozy evening treat or a festive brunch.

Recipe 58: Key Lime Pie

Savor the tangy zest of Key Lime Pie, which is brilliantly adapted for your air fryer. This diabetic-friendly version offers all the refreshing flavors you crave combined into a healthier, guilt-free dessert that's as satisfying as it is easy to make.

Prep Time: 20 minutes

Cook Time: 10 minutes

Serves: 4

Ingredients:

- ➢ 1 cup almond flour
- ➢ 2 tablespoons unsalted butter, melted
- ➢ 1/4 cup sugar substitute
- ➢ 3 large eggs
- ➢ 1/2 cup key lime juice

- ➢ 1 teaspoon lime zest
- ➢ 1/4 cup heavy cream

Instructions:

1. Mix almond flour, melted butter, and 1 tablespoon sugar substitute to form the crust. Press into a greased air fryer-safe pie dish.

2. Preheat the air fryer to 320°F (160°C).

3. Bake the crust for 5 minutes, then remove and let it cool.

4. Whisk the eggs, key lime juice, zest, heavy cream, and remaining sugar substitute. Pour the mixture over the crust.

5. Return to the air fryer and cook for 5 minutes or until set.

6. Chill in the refrigerator for at least 2 hours before serving.

Nutritional Facts (Per serving):

- ❖ Calories: 280
- ❖ Carbohydrates: 12g
- ❖ Protein: 9g
- ❖ Fat: 22g
- ❖ Fiber: 2g
- ❖ Sugar: 2g

Enjoy this delightful Key Lime Pie, a creamy, tangy dessert that brings a slice of tropical paradise to your table without straying from your healthy eating goals. It's perfect for a refreshing end to any meal!

Recipe 59: Potato Patties Deep Fry Crunchy Crispy

Dive into the irresistible crunch of Potato Patties, crafted to perfection in your air fryer for a crispy, golden exterior and a soft, fluffy interior. This diabetic-friendly snack offers a healthier twist on a beloved classic, ensuring guilt-free indulgence.

Prep Time: 15 minutes

Cook Time: 20 minutes

Serves: 4

Ingredients:

- 2 large potatoes, peeled and grated
- 1/4 cup onion, finely chopped
- 2 tablespoons almond flour
- 1 egg, beaten

- ➤ 1/2 teaspoon garlic powder
- ➤ Salt and pepper to taste
- ➤ Cooking spray

Instructions:

1. Squeeze excess moisture from the grated potatoes using a towel.
2. Mix potatoes, onion, almond flour, beaten egg, garlic powder, salt, and pepper in a bowl.
3. Form the mixture into small patties.
4. Preheat the air fryer to 390°F (200°C) and spray the basket with cooking spray.
5. Place the patties in the basket, ensuring they don't touch. Spray the tops with cooking spray.
6. Cook for 10 minutes, flip the patties, and cook for another 10 minutes until crispy and golden.
7. Serve hot.

Nutritional Facts (Per serving):

- ❖ Calories: 150
- ❖ Carbohydrates: 20g
- ❖ Protein: 4g
- ❖ Fat: 6g
- ❖ Fiber: 2g
- ❖ Sugar: 1g

Relish these Potato Patties, a delightful and easy snack perfect for satisfying your cravings while keeping your dietary needs in mind. They have a crispy exterior and tender heart, ideal for any occasion!

Recipe 60: Apple Pie with Cinnamon

Embrace the cozy warmth of Apple Pie with Cinnamon, perfectly baked in your air fryer. This diabetic-friendly version offers all the classic flavors you love—spiced apples enveloped in a flaky crust—without compromising your health goals.

Prep Time: 20 minutes

Cook Time: 15 minutes

Serves: 4

Ingredients:

- ➢ 2 large apples, peeled and sliced
- ➢ 1 teaspoon cinnamon
- ➢ 1/2 cup almond flour
- ➢ 1/4 cup sugar substitute
- ➢ 2 tablespoons unsalted butter

- ➢ 1 egg (for egg wash)
- ➢ Pinch of salt

Instructions:

1. Toss sliced apples with cinnamon and 2 tablespoons of sugar substitute.

2. Mix almond flour, remaining sugar substitute, salt, and butter in a bowl until crumbly.

3. Line a small air fryer-safe pie dish with half of the dough. Add the apple mixture. Top with remaining dough.

4. Brush with beaten egg for a golden finish.

5. Preheat the air fryer to 350°F (177°C).

6. Cook for 15 minutes or until the crust is golden and the apples are tender.

7. Let cool before serving.

Nutritional Facts (Per serving):

- ❖ Calories: 220
- ❖ Carbohydrates: 18g
- ❖ Protein: 5g
- ❖ Fat: 15g
- ❖ Fiber: 4g
- ❖ Sugar: 10g

Savor each bite of this Apple Pie with Cinnamon, a dessert that combines traditional comfort with modern health-conscious preparation. Perfect for a sweet, satisfying treat without the guilt.

Conclusion

As we conclude this culinary journey through "Effortless Diabetic Air Fryer Recipes for Beginners," we hope Delores Pyle's collection has enriched your kitchen repertoire and empowered you with the tools to manage diabetes confidently and pleasantly. Each recipe was designed to bring simplicity and joy back into your diet, proving that a diabetes-friendly lifestyle can be both delicious and uncomplicated.

Throughout this book, you've explored an array of dishes that showcase the versatility of the air fryer—from savory dinners to sweet treats—all tailored to support your health goals while satisfying your palate. The air fryer's ability to deliver tasty meals with less oil has hopefully inspired you to continue making healthier food choices that support your dietary needs.

We encourage you to revisit these recipes, experimenting with the flavors and customizing them to your taste. Cooking is not just about following recipes; it's about creating meals that resonate with your healthy journey and preferences. As you grow more comfortable with these dishes, let your creativity lead the way—adapt, modify, and innovate.

Remember, managing diabetes effectively does not require sacrificing the foods you love. With tools like this cookbook and your air fryer, you can continue to enjoy eating well while taking care of your body. We hope these recipes become a staple in your routine, bringing health, happiness, and ease to your table.

Thank you for choosing this guide to assist your journey toward a healthier life. May the simplicity and flavor of each recipe remind you that your dietary management can be as enjoyable as it is beneficial. Keep this cookbook close, for it is a collection of recipes and a companion in your ongoing quest for wellness.

19809073R00075